TEACHER'S MANUAL FOR

A Christmas Carol

THE GRAPHIC NOVEL

HEINLE
CENGAGE Learning™

Australia • Brazil • Japan • Korea • Mexico • Singapore • Spain • United Kingdom • United States

HEINLE
CENGAGE Learning

Teacher's Manual for A Christmas Carol: The Graphic Novel

Charles Dickens

Publisher: Sherrise Roehr

Managing Development Editor: John Hicks

Associate Development Editor: Cécile Engeln

Director of U.S. Marketing: Jim McDonough

Director of Global Marketing: Ian Martin

Assistant Marketing Manager: Jide Iruka

Associate Content Project Manager: Mark Rzeszutek

Print Buyer: Sue Spencer

Script by Sean Michael Wilson

Text Designer: Classical Comics Ltd.

Pencils: Mike Collins

Inks: David Roach

Coloring: James Offredi

Lettering: Terri Wiley

Compositor: MPS Limited, A Macmillan Company

Cover Designer: Gina Petti

ISBN 13: 978-1-4240-4632-4

ISBN 10: 1-4240-4632-7

Heinle
20 Channel Center Street
Boston, MA 02210
USA

Cengage Learning is a leading provider of customised learning solutions with office locations around the globe, including Singapore, the United Kingdom, Australia, Mexico, Brazil and Japan. Locate our local office at: **international.cengage.com/region**

Cengage Learning products are represented in Canada by Nelson Education, Ltd.

Visit Heinle online at **elt.heinle.com**

Visit our corporate website at **cengage.com**

CONTENTS

Introduction

Welcome to the Teacher's Manual for *A CHRISTMAS CAROL: THE GRAPHIC NOVEL*

This Teacher's Manual is structured to guide you and your students through reading and discussing *A Christmas Carol: The Graphic Novel*. The manual is divided into three sections: Before You Read, While You Read, and After You Read. Each section contains worksheets for students to complete as well as teacher's notes that explain the focus of the worksheet and provide answers and teaching suggestions.

The worksheets encourage students to expand and develop their English skills by working on reading, writing, listening, and speaking. Students will also develop valuable study skills such as note taking, organizing information, and reading for comprehension. There are three integrated quizzes, as well as two tests. Answer keys to the quizzes and tests can be found on pp. 56–59 of the Teacher's Manual.

The Teacher's Manual also has an appendix which lists Dickens's literary works and Web sites for further reading or research on Charles Dickens, the novella *A Christmas Carol*, and literature in the Victorian era.

First published in 1843, *A Christmas Carol* emerged during a time of huge social and economic change in England, and also during what could be called a "Christmas renaissance:" a period of nostalgia for and revival of long-forgotten Christmas traditions. While reading *A Christmas Carol: The Graphic Novel*, you may want to examine the following with students:

- labor laws and workers' rights
- poverty and social responsibility
- attitudes toward disabilities
- Christmas traditions
- the role of religion in society
- belief in ghosts/spirits

Ask students how attitudes and ideas have changed from the Victorian era to the modern age, and how they may differ from culture to culture.

The central themes in *A Christmas Carol* are mainly focused on the human spirit—its capacity for warmth and generosity as well as for selfishness and cruelty, but also its ability to change for the better. The theme is that people are more important than money, and kindness and generosity win out over greed and coldheartedness—particularly at Christmastime. It is a cautionary tale, but one of prevailing optimism.

A Christmas Carol remains one of the most beloved Christmas stories of all time. It has inspired countless TV, film, theatrical, and print adaptations and has influenced many others. Ebenezer Scrooge is one of the most recognizable literary figures associated with the Christmas season, a symbol of the heartless miser but also of the redeemed man who learns to love life and humanity. Its themes of social justice, forgiveness, redemption, compassion, and generosity are timeless, and its powerful lessons carry through to readers today.

Important Events in Charles Dickens's Life

Date	What Happened?
1812	Charles Dickens is born in Landport, England.
1822	The Dickens family moves to London.
1824	Dickens's father is arrested for debt, and the family moves to Marshalsea Prison with him. Dickens (age 12) is sent to work at a factory.
1827	Dickens becomes a law clerk.
1828	Dickens becomes a reporter for the *True Sun* newspaper.
1833	Dickens publishes his first story, "A Dinner at Poplar Walk."
1836	Dickens publishes his first novel, *The Pickwick Papers*. Dickens marries Catherine Hogarth.
1837	Dickens begins writing *Oliver Twist*. Catherine's younger sister dies.
1843	Dickens publishes *A Christmas Carol*.
1851	Dickens's father dies. Dickens's daughter, Dora, dies.
1857	Dickens performs for Queen Victoria. Dickens meets and falls in love with an actress named Ellen Lawless Ternan.
1858	Dickens separates from his wife, Catherine.
1863	Dickens's mother dies. Dickens's son, Walter, dies in India.
1865	Dickens is in the Staplehurst Railway Accident.
1870	Dickens dies of a stroke and is buried at Westminster Abbey. Dickens leaves his last novel, *The Mystery of Edwin Drood*, unfinished.

See pp. 149–150 of *A Christmas Carol: The Graphic Novel* for a more complete timeline of Charles Dickens's life.

Teacher's notes

Worksheet 1

This worksheet introduces Charles Dickens and the major events of his life. Many of these events shaped the themes in his writing.

Have students look at the timeline of Charles Dickens's life on p. 3 of the Teacher's Manual, and on p. 27 of the Workbook.

Make sure that students understand the words *debt* and *stroke*.

- *Debt* is a sum of money you owe to someone—it could be to a person, or to a bank, a government, or a company.
- A *stroke* happens when a blood vessel in someone's brain bursts or becomes blocked, which may kill them or make them unable to move one side of their body.

Discussion question: What happened when Dickens was 12 years old? How do you think he felt about that? What effect do you think this had on Dickens and his writing? (Sample answer: Dickens's father was arrested for debt, and the whole family moved to prison with him. Dickens went to work in a blacking factory. This was probably very embarrassing for the family, and very difficult for Dickens. It probably made him think a lot about what happens to people who have no money and about the conditions that they have to live and work in.)

A. Have students look at the list of events. Ask them to put the events in order without looking at the timeline. Then, have students read the full biography of Dickens on pp. 147–148 of *A Christmas Carol: The Graphic Novel.* Have students check their answers. They can also look at the detailed timeline on pp. 149–150 of the graphic novel.

ANSWER KEY: 1. d; **2.** h; **3.** f; **4.** e; **5.** a; **6.** c; **7.** b; **8.** g

B. Once students have read the biography and the full timeline in the graphic novel, have students read the statements and decide if they are true or false. Let them refer back to the information in the book to find the answers. Once they have circled "True" or "False," go over the statements orally as a class, and have students correct the false statements.

ANSWER KEY: 1. False. Dickens was born in Landport, England, in 1812. **2.** True; **3.** True; **4.** False. He met Ellen Lawless Ternan in 1857, but he didn't marry her. He married Catherine Hogarth in 1836 and separated from her in 1858. **5.** False. Dickens had a mild stroke in 1869, but he did not die from the stroke until 1870. **6.** False. He was buried in Westminster Abbey, not at Gads Hill. **7.** False. Dickens never finished his novel *The Mystery of Edwin Drood.* It appeared after his death, but it was unfinished.

C. The answers to these questions can be found in the author biography and the detailed timeline. Direct students to pp. 147–150 of the graphic novel to find the answers.

ANSWER KEY: 1. *The Pickwick Papers, Oliver Twist, Nicholas Nickleby, The Old Curiosity Shop, Dombey and Son, The Haunted Man, David Copperfield, Bleak House, Hard Times, Little Dorrit, Great Expectations,* and *Our Mutual Friend.* (Note: *Sketches by Boz* does not count. It is described as a collection of articles, not a novel.) **2.** Dickens wanted a simple and private funeral. His funeral was private but not simple because he was very popular. People wanted him to be buried at Westminster Abbey. However, his grave is simple, with only a stone that shows his name, his date of birth, and date of death.

Name: ____________________

Before You Read

Worksheet 1 – Meet Charles Dickens

A. Look at the following events from Dickens's life. Put the events in the correct order.

1. ______	**a.** Dickens publishes *A Christmas Carol.*
2. ______	**b.** Dickens is in a major railway accident.
3. ______	**c.** Dickens meets and falls in love with Ellen Lawless Ternan.
4. ______	**d.** Dickens goes to work in a factory.
5. ______	**e.** Dickens marries Catherine Hogarth.
6. ______	**f.** Dickens publishes his first story, "A Dinner at Poplar Walk."
7. ______	**g.** Dickens has a stroke.
8. ______	**h.** Dickens gets a job at the *True Sun* newspaper.

B. Read the following statements. Decide whether they are True or False. Circle your answers.

1. Dickens was born in London, England, in 1812. True False

   ____

2. Dickens had a job as a law clerk at age 15. True False

   ____

3. Dickens used the name "Boz" to publish articles in the *Morning Chronicle.* True False

   ____

4. Dickens met and married Ellen Lawless Ternan in 1857. True False

   ____

5. Dickens died of a stroke in 1869. True False

   ____

6. He was buried at Gads Hill. True False

   ____

7. Dickens's last novel, *The Mystery of Edwin Drood,* was published after his death. True False

   ____

C. Answer the questions about Dickens, based on the biography on pp. 147–150 and timelines you read.

1. What are three novels, besides *A Christmas Carol,* that Dickens wrote?

   ____

   ____

2. What kind of funeral did Dickens want? Did his family respect his wishes? Explain.

   ____

   ____

   ____

   ____

   ____

Teacher's Notes

Worksheet 2

This worksheet focuses on information from "Hard Times" and "A Very Victorian Christmas" on pp. 151–155 of *A Christmas Carol: The Graphic Novel.* Students should read these selections before reading the graphic novel to get a better sense of what life and society were like in Dickens's—and Scrooge's—time.

Before doing Worksheet 2, break the class into two groups. One group will read "Hard Times," and the other will read "A Very Victorian Christmas." Each group will work together to **summarize** the assigned reading. Explain that a **summary** is a short account of a reading, which gives the main points but not the details. For "Hard Times," you might ask students to write one sentence to summarize each paragraph. For "A Very Victorian Christmas," summaries could be done by section (there are five sections). Ask each group to present their summaries to the class.

A. This activity summarizes information from "Hard Times" and "A Very Victorian Christmas" while practicing some new vocabulary. Make sure students are familiar with the vocabulary words before proceeding. Tell students to find each word in the glossary and then use it in a sentence. (Note: "Industrial Revolution" is not in the glossary. Students can get the definition from reading "Hard Times.")

ANSWER KEY: 1. Industrial Revolution; **2.** travel; **3.** carriage; **4.** suffered; **5.** parliament; **6.** celebrate; **7.** afford; **8.** feast; **9.** provide; **10.** charity

Discussion question: How did the Industrial Revolution benefit English society? How did it hurt English society? (Sample answer: The Industrial Revolution introduced many important inventions that made life easier for people, like the steam engine, the railroad, the telephone, and the postal service. However, it also created terrible living conditions for poor people. As the population grew, people moved to the cities for jobs. This created slums. Workers were often not paid very much and worked in dangerous conditions. Many children were forced to work.)
Note: Explain that Dickens was very troubled by the developments of the Industrial Revolution. Most of his novels criticize the poverty and the pollution that resulted from it.

B. The multiple choice questions in this activity are also based on the two readings on the Victorian era. Again, allow students to check the readings to find the answers.

ANSWER KEY: 1. a (see p. 153, first paragraph); **2.** c (see p. 152, third paragraph; p. 155, first paragraph); **3.** b (see p. 154, first paragraph); **4.** b (see p. 151, second column, second paragraph)

Name: ____

Before You Read

Worksheet 2 – Dickens's World: The Victorian Era

A. Read about the Victorian era on pp. 151–155 of *A Christmas Carol: The Graphic Novel.* Then complete the paragraph below using the words in the word bank.

charity	celebrate	afford	Industrial Revolution	suffered
travel	carriage	feast	parliament	provide

The Victorian Era and Christmas

The Victorian era was a time of many changes in England. The 1. ______________ brought many new developments in technology, like the steam engine, the telephone, and factory production. New railroads made it easier for people to 2. ______________ long distances. But people who lived in cities still used a horse and 3. ______________ to get around. Middle-class and upper-class people benefited from these changes, but poor, working-class people 4. ______________. Many poor people lived and worked in bad conditions. Many children had to work in factories. The 5. ______________ passed laws to protect children, but life was still difficult.

Before the Victorian era, most English people did not 6. ______________ Christmas. It became popular again under Queen Victoria. However, most poor people still did not get the day off from work and could not 7. ______________ to buy gifts or food for a 8. ______________. Queen Victoria thought it was important to 9. ______________ food and clothing for poor people during Christmastime. Following her example, people began to give to 10. ______________.

B. Complete each statement by circling the correct answer.

1. "Yule" was _____.
   - **a.** a midwinter festival celebrated before Christianity came to Europe
   - **b.** the day after Christmas; a day to give gifts to the poor
   - **c.** a royal celebration in Queen Victoria's family
2. Dickens, and many other people, believed that _____ was the solution to problems of crime and poverty.
   - **a.** charity
   - **b.** a law passed by parliament
   - **c.** education
3. The first Christmas card was created by _____ in 1843.
   - **a.** Dickens
   - **b.** Sir Henry Cole, a businessman
   - **c.** Queen Charlotte, Victoria's grandmother
4. The population of Great Britain _____ between 1800 and 1900.
   - **a.** doubled
   - **b.** tripled
   - **c.** did not grow

Teacher's Notes

Worksheet 3

This worksheet introduces some of the elements of fiction. Ask students to name short stories that they have read. Ask what novels they have read. Explain that a novella is a short novel, but it is longer than a short story. The same literary elements apply to all three types of fiction.

A. Ask students to look at the literary terms and talk about the ones they already know. Then, have them read the definitions and match them to the correct literary elements.

Discussion questions:

- Think of a story (or movie) you know. Who is the main character? What is the conflict? What happens at the climax? (Answers will vary.)
- What usually happens *after* the climax of a story? (In this part of the story, we see what happens to the characters after the conflict is resolved.)

Note: Explain that the conflict or conflicts in a story create **tension** (a feeling of anxiety produced by a difficult or dangerous situation). The climax is where the tension reaches its highest point, and then breaks. The conflict is resolved.

ANSWER KEY: 1. f; **2.** b; **3.** e; **4.** d; **5.** c; **6.** a; **7.** g

B. Next, students will identify specific elements from *A Christmas Carol: The Graphic Novel.* Explain that a novella can have more than one setting, more than one mood, and more than one theme.

ANSWER KEY:

character	plot	setting	mood	theme
Mrs. Cratchit the Ghost of Christmas Past	Fred visits Scrooge Scrooge sees a ghost	Scrooge's office Christmas Eve	warm merry cold gloomy	the dangers of greed the struggles of poverty

C. Students will complete this activity as they read, or after they have read *A Christmas Carol: The Graphic Novel.* Revisit this activity when you have finished the graphic novel as a class.

As an additional activity, have students keep a chapter-by-chapter log of all the literary elements. Which characters appear? What are the different settings and moods? What are the main plot points? Students can note this information in a table, chart, or on index cards by chapter. Have them note which chapter the climax occurs in.

Note: Explain that in literature, there are generally two types of conflict: **external conflict** and **internal conflict**. The common types of external conflict are *man vs. man* (the main character's goal is in opposition to another character's goal), *man vs. society*, or *man vs. nature* (the character's main obstacle to reaching his or her goal is society or nature). An internal conflict is *man vs. himself* (the main character has an internal struggle with his or her own mind or personality). In *A Christmas Carol,* the conflict is internal (man vs. himself); Scrooge's distaste for poverty has turned him into a greedy, stingy, miserable man. He must realize this and change in order to find happiness.

SAMPLE ANSWERS: 1. The major conflict is between Scrooge and himself, as he begins to realize how his behavior has hurt people, including himself. **2.** The climax of the story is when Scrooge is with the Ghost of Christmas to Come. He realizes that he has caused a lot of misery and that he will die alone and hated unless he changes his ways. **3.** The main theme of the book is that money isn't everything (or, money isn't as important as friends and family; or, it's better to be generous than stingy).

Name: ____

Before You Read

Worksheet 3 – Prepare to Discuss the Novella

A. Match the elements of a novella with their definitions.

1. _____ character	**a.**	the most dramatic point of the story, just before the end
2. _____ setting	**b.**	the time and place in which a story happens
3. _____ plot	**c.**	the feeling or the atmosphere
4. _____ theme	**d.**	an idea in the story that the author wants to communicate
5. _____ mood	**e.**	the events of a story
6. _____ climax	**f.**	a person in the story
7. _____ conflict	**g.**	the main problem or struggle

B. The words and phrases in the word bank describe elements from *A Christmas Carol: The Graphic Novel.* Put each word or phrase in the correct category.

Mrs. Cratchit	Fred visits Scrooge	warm	gloomy
the Ghost of Christmas Past	Scrooge's office	Christmas Eve	merry
Scrooge sees a ghost	the struggles of poverty	the dangers of greed	cold

character	plot	setting	mood	theme

C. As you read *A Christmas Carol: The Graphic Novel,* fill in the blanks below with information about each element.

1. major conflict: ____

____

2. climax: ____

____

3. main theme: ____

____

Teacher's Notes
Worksheet 4

This worksheet provides a synopsis of Chapter One of *A Christmas Carol: The Graphic Novel* to prepare students for what they will read. It also practices some of the vocabulary from the story.

A. Ask students to fill in the blanks with the words from the word bank. If they are not sure of the meaning of a word, encourage them to look it up in the glossary. And then try it in a sentence and see if it "fits." If they are still not sure, have them continue with the activity until all the words are used. They will probably discover where the word should go through process of elimination.

Alternately, the words can be practiced as a class before beginning the activity.

ANSWER KEY: **1.** stingy; **2.** generous; **3.** donate; **4.** be left alone; **5.** take care of; **6.** crutch; **7.** nephew; **8.** feast; **9.** observe; **10.** complains; **11.** coldhearted; **12.** ghosts; **13.** journey; **14.** lesson

Discussion question: Can you **predict** what will happen when the ghosts visit Scrooge? (Answers will vary.)

Note: Some students might already be familiar with the story. Before you ask this question, ask the class if anyone has read or seen an adaptation of this story. If any students raise their hands, ask them not to give away the story to the other students, and to let the students who don't know the story guess what will happen.

B. This activity reviews the material covered in Worksheet 3 and prepares students to begin reading the story. Ask them to turn to p. 7 in the graphic novel and study the images. Encourage them to concentrate on the pictures, not the words.

ANSWER KEY: **1.** a churchyard or graveyard at night; **2.** old gravestones, a church, snow, dead trees, birds flying, the grave of Jacob Marley; **3.** dark, creepy, scary, ominous, serious

Name: ______________________________

Before You Read

Worksheet 4 – The Story

A. Read the summary of Chapter One. Fill in the blanks with words from the word bank.

nephew	complains	generous	crutch	observe	journey	lesson
take care of	be left alone	donate	feast	stingy	coldhearted	ghosts

Ebenezer Scrooge is a 1. ____________________ old miser. He has a lot of money, but he doesn't spend it. He is not a 2. ____________________ man. He doesn't 3. ____________________ money to poor people or give gifts to his family and friends. In fact, he doesn't have any friends. Nobody likes Scrooge, but he doesn't care. He prefers to 4. ____________________ with his money.

Bob Cratchit works for Scrooge. Scrooge doesn't pay Bob a lot of money, even though he must 5. ____________________ a large family. Bob has a small son named Tiny Tim. Tiny Tim can't walk, so he uses a 6. ____________________ to help him. Although he is sick, he is a very happy child.

The story begins on Christmas Eve. Scrooge and Bob are working in the office. Scrooge's 7. ____________________, Fred, visits the office to say "Merry Christmas." He invites Scrooge to his Christmas 8. ____________________. Scrooge is not interested. He does not 9. ____________________ the Christmas holiday. Scrooge even 10. ____________________ when Bob asks for the day off!

Scrooge is a mean, 11. ____________________ man who does not care about others. But that evening, everything will change for him. He will be visited by four 12. ____________________ who will take him on a 13. ____________________ through time and space. Will Scrooge learn a valuable 14. ____________________?

B. Now, turn to p. 7 in *A Christmas Carol: The Graphic Novel* for a preview of what you will read. Look at the pictures. Then answer the following questions.

1. What is the setting?

   ____

2. What do you see in the pictures?

   ____

3. What is the mood?

   ____

Teacher's notes
Worksheet 5

The purpose of this worksheet is to introduce some of the major and minor characters from the story.

A. In this activity, students will cut out the images of the characters, and match them to the names and descriptions.

Direct students first to pp. 4–5 of *A Christmas Carol: The Graphic Novel.* Without giving away too much of the story, explain who the characters are and what their relationship is to Scrooge. For example, Fred is Scrooge's nephew.

Introduce or review some of the vocabulary words needed to talk about the characters: *coldhearted, merry, lame, ghost, miser, clerk, undertaker, funeral.*

Note: Not all of the characters from pp. 4–5 are included in the cut-out activity.

Discussion question: After looking at the pictures of the characters, explain what kind of story you think this will be (e.g., sad, sentimental, happy/merry, funny, scary, educational). Why? (Sample answer: It looks like the story will be a little scary, a little sad, and happy, too. Two of the ghosts look scary, and Scrooge's face looks scared. So, I think some parts of the story will be scary. Some of the characters, like Belle and Caroline, look sad. Also, there is an undertaker in the story, so some parts are probably sad. But some of the characters are smiling and laughing, and the story is about Christmas, so it will probably have happy parts, too.)

Note: Revisit this question after students have read the whole story, and have students compare their first impressions with their final impressions.

ANSWER KEY:

The Ghosts

1 
Ghost of Jacob Marley
Scrooge's old partner

2 
Ghost of Christmas Past

3 
Ghost of Christmas Present

4 
Ghost of Christmas to Come

The Present

5 
Ebenezer Scrooge
coldhearted miser

6 
Bob Cratchit
Scrooge's clerk

7 
Mrs. Cratchit

8 
Tiny Tim Cratchit
Bob's youngest son, who is lame

9 
Fred
Scrooge's merry nephew

10 
Alice
Fred's wife

The Past

11 
Fan
Scrooge's sister

12 
Mr. and Mrs. Fezziwig
Scrooge's boss and his wife

13 
Belle
Scrooge's old love

The Future

14 
Old Joe
Shop owner

15 
Undertaker

16 
Caroline
a poor woman and her husband

Name: ______________________________

Before You Read

Worksheet 5 – Meet the Characters

A. Cut out the faces. Then glue or tape them in the correct spaces below.

The Ghosts

Ghost of Jacob Marley
Scrooge's old partner

Ghost of Christmas Past

Ghost of Christmas Present

Ghost of Christmas to Come

The Present

Ebenezer Scrooge
coldhearted miser

Bob Cratchit
Scrooge's clerk

Mrs. Cratchit

Tiny Tim Cratchit
Bob's youngest son, who is lame

Fred
Scrooge's merry nephew

Alice
Fred's wife

The Past

Fan
Scrooge's sister

Mr. and Mrs. Fezziwig
Scrooge's boss and his wife

Belle
Scrooge's old love

The Future

Old Joe
Shop owner

Undertaker

Caroline
a poor woman and her husband

Cutouts for Worksheet 5 – Meet the Characters

Cut out the faces. Glue or tape them in the correct places on Worksheet 5.

1

2

3

4

5

6

7

8

9

10

11

12

13

14

15

16

Name: ____________________

Quiz 1
Worksheets 1–5

A. Match the characters' names with their descriptions.

1. _____	Mr. Fezziwig	**a.**	Scrooge's sister
2. _____	Tiny Tim	**b.**	Scrooge's nephew; a kind and merry man
3. _____	Bob Cratchit	**c.**	A lame boy; the youngest Cratchit child
4. _____	Fan	**d.**	Scrooge's dead business partner, now a ghost
5. _____	Belle	**e.**	Scrooge's clerk; a poor man
6. _____	Fred	**f.**	Scrooge's old boss
7. _____	Jacob Marley	**g.**	a girl Scrooge loved when he was young

B. Unscramble the words and names to fit the descriptions. Don't forget to capitalize names, titles, and places.

1. Dickens's first novel	het ickpickw spaerp ____________
2. Dickens is buried here.	etsmwinerts babye ____________
3. It was a period of social and economic change in England (1837–1901).	itcvronia rae ____________
4. Dickens's father went to prison for this.	bedt ____________
5. The Industrial Revolution created wealth for the rich but worsened _______ for the poor.	vetropy ____________

C. Write the name of the correct element of a novella next to each definition.

1. where and when a story takes place: ____________
2. the main problem in the story: ____________
3. an important idea in the story: ____________
4. what happens in the story: ____________
5. one of the people in the story: ____________
6. how the story feels; the atmosphere: ____________
7. the most exciting part of the story: ____________

Teacher's Notes
Worksheet 6

Before starting the graphic novel, read the introduction to the story on p. 6 as a class. The introduction contains some of the ideas presented in "A Very Victorian Christmas" on pp. 153–155. After reading the first three paragraphs, ask students to name some Christmas traditions in the United States and in other countries. How are they similar or different from celebrations in the Victorian era? Then, read the last paragraph. Ask students to answer the last question. Do they think it is possible for someone who is cold and selfish to change? Why or why not?

If students have never read a graphic novel before, point out the difference between the square boxes that indicate narration (see p. 7) and the speech bubbles that indicate dialogue (see p. 12).

Track 2

A. First, have students read Chapter One, pp. 7–9, as they listen to the audio. Ask students to correct the false statements orally as a class.

ANSWER KEY: **1.** True; **2.** True; **3.** False. He never removed Marley's name; **4.** False. No one talks to Scrooge on the street, and he likes it that way; **5.** False. He is coldhearted and frozen on the inside.

Track 3

B. Have students read Chapter One, pp. 10–12, as they listen to the audio. Then have them answer the questions.

ANSWER KEY: **1.** b; **2.** c; **3.** a

Track 4

C. Have students read and listen to Chapter One, pp. 13–16, stopping after Scrooge says, "The world's gone crazy." in the second row. Then have them answer the questions.

SAMPLE ANSWERS: **1.** Scrooge thinks Christmas is ridiculous. He doesn't understand how poor people can feel happy at this time of year. He can't understand how something that doesn't make money can make anyone happy. Scrooge himself is not happy, even though he has plenty of money. His nephew, Fred, thinks Christmas is a time when people are kinder and gentler. Fred does not think that money is related to happiness. Fred is a happy person who likes to celebrate and share with his family and friends. **2.** Bob agrees with Fred about Christmas. This is obvious because he smiles and claps after Fred gives a speech about how good Christmas is.

Discussion question: On p. 15, Scrooge asks Fred about his marriage. Why did he ask this question? What is Scrooge's attitude toward Fred's marriage? Why? (Sample answer: Scrooge's attitude is condescending and sarcastic. He thinks it is ridiculous for people to get married because they fall in love. Maybe this is because he is coldhearted and can't remember what it's like to love another person.)

Note: Revisit this scene after students read the section in Chapter Two, pp. 61–65, where Scrooge sees Belle, the woman he was going to marry. Ask students if there is a deeper reason for Scrooge's hostile attitude toward his nephew on p. 15.

D. This activity summarizes the first part of Chapter One and practices some of the new vocabulary.

ANSWER KEY: **1.** miser; **2.** coldhearted; **3.** allow; **4.** observe; **5.** merry; **6.** bless

Name: ____

While You Read

Worksheet 6 – Chapter One: Marley's Ghost, pp. 7–16

Track 2

A. Read Chapter One, pp. 7–9, while you listen to the audio. Decide if the following statements are True or False. Circle your answer.

1. Scrooge's partner, Jacob Marley, is dead.	True	False
2. Scrooge is the only person who went to Marley's funeral.	True	False
3. Scrooge removes Marley's name from the sign on his office.	True	False
4. Scrooge likes to talk to people he meets on the street.	True	False
5. Scrooge seems unfriendly, but inside he has a warm and merry heart.	True	False

Track 3

B. Read Chapter One, pp. 10–12, while you listen to the audio. Then circle the best word or phrase to complete each sentence.

1. The setting of this chapter is _____.

a. Christmas Day
b. Christmas Eve
c. a week before Christmas

2. Scrooge allows Bob to have only a tiny fire because _____.

a. Bob is not cold and does not need a large fire
b. Scrooge doesn't have enough money to buy more coal for a larger fire
c. Scrooge is a miser and does not want to pay for more coal

3. When Scrooge says "Bah, humbug!" to Fred, it means that _____.

a. he thinks Christmas is ridiculous
b. he thinks his nephew is lying to him and does not really wish him a merry Christmas
c. he thinks only rich people should celebrate Christmas

Track 4

C. Listen to the audio as you read Chapter One, pp. 13–16. Then answer the questions.

1. How does Scrooge feel about Christmas? How does his nephew feel? Compare their attitudes.

____
____
____

2. Does Bob agree with Scrooge or Fred? How do you know?

____
____

D. Use the words from the word bank to complete the summary.

observe	bless	allow	miser	merry	coldhearted

Scrooge is rich, but he keeps his money for himself. He is a **1.** ______________ . He is so **2.** ______________ that he will not even **3.** ______________ his clerk, Bob, to have a large fire to keep him warm. Fred, Scrooge's nephew, invites Scrooge to Christmas dinner. But Scrooge does not **4.** ______________ Christmas. He doesn't understand why Fred is so **5.** ______________ if he is poor. Fred says that things don't have to make money to be good. Fred loves Christmas, and he says, "God **6.** ______________ it!"

Teacher's Notes

Worksheet 7

Track 5

A. This activity reviews Chapter One, pp. 16–19, and practices vocabulary words from these pages. Have students listen to the audio as they read Chapter One, pp. 16–19. Then have them identify the words based on the underlined definitions in the sentences.

ANSWER KEY: 1. charity; **2.** generous; **3.** necessities; **4.** donate; **5.** anonymously; **6.** prisons

Discussion question: Do you think the government has a responsibility to take care of poor people, or is it the responsibility of charities and generous people? Do you think the wealthy have an obligation to help poor people? Explain your opinion and give examples. (Answers will vary.)

Track 6

B. This activity reviews Chapter One, pp. 20–28. Students should read and listen to the section before they read the statements and do the activity. Then they can check their answers as they read and listen again.

ANSWER KEY: 1. d; **2.** c; **3.** e; **4.** b; **5.** a; **6.** h; **7.** i; **8.** j; **9.** g; **10.** f

Tracks 5–6

C. This last activity reviews the events of Chapter One, pp. 16–28. Have students read and listen to the section again before they complete the chart.

ANSWER KEY: 1. Scrooge doesn't want to give anything. He asks if there are prisons and workhouses for the poor. **2.** Scrooge says that if poor people want to die they should "hurry up and do it." **3.** Scrooge agrees to give Bob the day off because he has to, but he is not happy about it. He says it is not fair that he has to pay Bob for a day he doesn't work. He also tells Bob to come in extra early the following day. **4.** Scrooge is really scared, but he tries to act like he isn't. He says "Bah, humbug!" as if he doesn't believe what he sees. He checks around the whole house to make sure everything is where it should be. He locks the door.

Discussion question: How do Scrooge's reactions to the events in the chart show what kind of person he is? (Sample answer: Scrooge's reaction to the charity collectors shows how greedy and selfish he is. He does not care what happens to poor people. He thinks they are lazy, and he doesn't have to help them. He doesn't even care if they die. In fact, he says that they should die! Scrooge's reaction to Bob also shows that he is greedy and selfish. He thinks that it's unfair to pay Bob for a day he does not work, even if it's only one day a year. He compares it to robbery. Scrooge's reaction to the strange events in his house show that he has weaknesses. This is the first time we see him not strong, not hard, and not cold. He is scared. Maybe this shows that he is human and can be influenced after all.)

Name: ______________________________

While You Read

Worksheet 7 – Chapter One: Marley's Ghost, pp. 16–28

Track 5

A. Listen to the audio as you read Chapter One, pp. 16–19. Then, read each statement below. Write the word from the word bank that means the same thing as the underlined word or phrase.

generous	anonymously	donate	necessities	prisons	~~charity~~

1. ___charity___ Two men arrive at Scrooge's office. They are collecting money for <u>an organization that raises money to help people who are very poor</u>.
2. __________ One of the men says he is sure that Mr. Scrooge is just as <u>giving</u> as Mr. Marley was.
3. __________ He says that many poor people do not have the basic <u>things that they need</u>.
4. __________ The two men want Scrooge to <u>give</u> money to the poor.
5. __________ One of the men asks Scrooge if he wants to give money <u>without letting people know that he is the person who did it.</u>
6. __________ Scrooge thinks that poor people should be in workhouses or <u>buildings where criminals are kept as punishment</u>.

Track 6

B. Read Chapter One, pp. 20–28, and listen to the audio. Then put the following events in the order they happened in the story.

1. ___e___
2. ______
3. ______
4. ______
5. ______
6. ______
7. ______
8. ______
9. ______
10. ______

a. Scrooge thinks he sees a hearse as he climbs the stairs.
b. Scrooge sees Marley's face on his door knocker.
c. Scrooge eats dinner.
d. Scrooge agrees to give Bob Christmas Day off.
e. Scrooge goes home.
f. Scrooge hears the sound of footsteps and chains on the stairs. He is scared.
g. Scrooge hears Marley's old servant bell ringing.
h. Scrooge checks to make sure everything in the house is in place.
i. Scrooge locks the door.
j. Scrooge sees Marley's face in the pictures on the wall.

Tracks 5–6

C. Now, reread Chapter One, pp. 16–28, as you listen to the audio again. Think about what happens and how Scrooge reacts. Fill in the following chart with Scrooge's reaction to each event.

What happens?	Scrooge's Reaction
1. Charity collectors ask for donations.	
2. A charity collector says that many poor people would rather die than go to prison or a workhouse.	
3. Bob asks if he can take Christmas Day off.	
4. Scrooge sees and hears strange things in his house.	

Teacher's Notes

Worksheet 8

This worksheet covers the last part of Chapter One.

Track 7

A. Have students listen to the audio as they read Chapter One, pp. 29–34. Then have them circle the word or phrase that correctly completes each statement.

ANSWER KEY: 1. doesn't believe; **2.** chain; **3.** eyes; **4.** sick; **5.** enjoy life; **6.** travel

Discussion questions:

- Do you think Scrooge recognizes Marley's ghost when he first arrives? (Answers will vary. Yes, Scrooge seems to recognize Marley's ghost.)
- Explain your answer. (At the bottom of p. 28, Scrooge says "I know that man...")
- If Scrooge recognizes Marley, why does Scrooge ask him who he is? (Because Scrooge can't believe that Marley is really there; he doesn't believe his eyes.)
- What does Marley do to finally convince Scrooge that he is really there? (He rises up into the air, shakes his chains, and moans and groans.)

Track 8

B. This activity reviews Chapter One, pp. 35–41, and practices vocabulary words from these pages. Have students listen to the audio as they read. Then have them identify the words based on the underlined definitions in the sentences.

ANSWER KEY: 1. cheer up; **2.** regret; **3.** make up for; **4.** bound; **5.** journeys; **6.** suffers; **7.** avoid; **8.** ghosts

Review vocabulary words with students. Ask:

- When would you need to *cheer* someone *up*? What could you do to cheer up a friend? A child? What cheers you up when you feel sad?
- Is there anything you *regret*? What?
- If you miss class, how can you *make up for it*? Suppose you have a bad experience in a restaurant. How could the restaurant *make up for it*?
- Describe a *journey* you have taken.
- What is something everyone should *avoid*? Why?
- Do you know any *ghost* stories? Do you believe in ghosts?

Tracks 7–8

C. This activity reviews Chapter One, pp. 29–41. Have students answer the questions in complete sentences.

SAMPLE ANSWERS: 1. The chain is the result of Marley's behavior in life. Instead of enjoying life, he worked to make money. He was not kind or generous. Each link of the chain represents an unkind action or a day of his life wasted in his office. Scrooge lives this way, so when he dies he will have the same punishment as Marley. **2.** Marley feels regret for the life he did not enjoy. He regrets choosing business over people. He wishes that he had loved Christmas more. He wishes he had left the office and traveled while he was alive. His punishment is to carry his chain and travel the world. There is no rest and no sleep, and he has to watch happy people live their lives. **3.** Marley tells Scrooge that he can avoid the same punishment. He tells Scrooge that three ghosts will visit him, and that Scrooge will have a chance to change his future.

Name: ____

While You Read

Worksheet 8 – Chapter One: Marley's Ghost, pp. 29–41

Track 7

A. Read and listen to Chapter One, pp. 29–34. Circle the word or phrase that correctly completes each statement below.

1. At first, Scrooge **believes/doesn't believe** that Marley's ghost is real.
2. Marley's ghost is carrying a **chain/toothpick**.
3. Scrooge says that he can't trust his **friends/eyes**.
4. Scrooge thinks that he might be **sick/dreaming**.
5. Marley's ghost says that everyone should **make money/enjoy life** before they die.
6. Now that Marley is dead, he has to **rest/travel**.

Track 8

B. Read Chapter One, pp. 35–41, and listen. Replace the underlined phrase in each sentence with a word from the word bank.

avoid	suffers	regret	ghosts	journeys	cheer up	bound	make up for

1. ______________ Marley can't say anything to help Scrooge stop feeling sad and become happy.
2. ______________ Marley feels sadness and disappointment for the way he lived his life.
3. ______________ Now, nothing can replace or compensate for the life that he lost.
4. ______________ Marley is tied to many heavy chains.
5. ______________ Marley has to make many long trips with his heavy chains.
6. ______________ Marley is badly affected by his situation, especially at Christmas.
7. ______________ Scrooge hopes that he can take action to prevent the suffering that Marley is experiencing.
8. ______________ Marley tells Scrooge that three spirits will visit him.

Tracks 7–8

C. Read Chapter One, pp. 29–41, again as you listen. Then answer the following questions about the story.

1. What does Marley's chain represent? Marley says that he made each link himself. And Marley tells Scrooge that Scrooge has been making a heavy chain for himself. What does he mean?

____

____

____

____

2. Why does Marley feel regret? What is his punishment for the life he lived?

____

____

3. What words of hope does Marley offer to Scrooge?

____

____

____

____

Teacher's Notes
Worksheet 9

Track 9

A. Have students read Chapter Two, pp. 42–48, as they listen to the audio. Have students read the True/False statements silently and circle their answers. Then go over the activity together as a class. Ask students to correct the false statements orally.

ANSWER KEY: 1. False. It is 12 o'clock. **2.** True; **3.** False. This ghost does not carry a chain. It carries a cap. **4.** False. Scrooge asks the ghost to put on its cap. **5.** True; **6.** True; **7.** False. The ghost says it's there for Scrooge's well-being. **8.** True

Discussion questions:

- What do you think the Ghost of Christmas Past will show Scrooge? (Scenes and people from Scrooge's past.)
- What do you think the Ghost of Christmas Past's cap represents? On p. 47, the ghost says "People like you made this cap for me and force me to wear it all the time!" Explain. (Sample answer: The cap would hide the ghost's light. People like Scrooge want to forget about their past, so the cap is a way of blocking out past memories.)

Note: Point out the shape of the ghost's cap (see p. 45). Students may not recognize the shape. It is supposed to look like a candle extinguisher. Explain that before electric light, when everyone used candles, people would put out the flame of candles with an extinguisher. *Extinguish* means to stop a fire from burning, or to stop a light from shining.

Track 10

B. Have students read Chapter Two, pp. 49–53, as they listen to the audio. Then, have students fill in the missing information in the statements. Replay the audio as they reread the section and correct their statements and/or fill in any blanks. Then go over the statements as a class.

SAMPLE ANSWERS: 1. grew up; **2.** small town; **3.** (alone) in the empty school; **4.** feels sad; **5.** the books/stories he read (as if they were real); **6.** singing a Christmas carol outside his office; give him money

Track 11

C. Have students read Chapter Two, pp. 54–61, as they listen to the audio. Stop reading at the second row on p. 61. Ask students to notice Scrooge's reaction to each character as they appear. Then have them fill in the chart with descriptions of each character and how Scrooge feels about them.

Character	Description/Action	How Scrooge Feels About Him/Her
Fan	Scrooge's sister; kind, cheerful; comes to bring Scrooge home for Christmas	He loves her and is happy to see her.
Mr. Fezziwig	Scrooge's boss; very generous and happy; gives a Christmas party for his employees	Scrooge likes him very much. He remembers how much he enjoyed the party.
Dick Wilkins	young man; Scrooge's coworker	Scrooge is happy to see his old friend.

Tracks 9–11

D. This activity reviews vocabulary words that appear in this section of Chapter Two. Have students match the words with the definitions.

ANSWER KEY: 1. e; **2.** d; **3.** h; **4.** b; **5.** i; **6.** f; **7.** c; **8.** a; **9.** g; **10.** k; **11.** j

Name: ______________________________

While You Read

Worksheet 9 – Chapter Two: The First Ghost, pp. 42–61

Track 9

A. Read Chapter Two, pp. 42–48, as you listen. Decide if the statements below are True or False. Circle your answer.

1.	When Scrooge wakes up, it is 1 o'clock.	True	False
2.	The Ghost of Christmas Past has a bright light shining from its head.	True	False
3.	This ghost also carries a heavy chain.	True	False
4.	Scrooge asks the ghost to put on its robe.	True	False
5.	The ghost is annoyed because Scrooge wants it to cover its light.	True	False
6.	This ghost is cheerful.	True	False
7.	The ghost says it is there to punish Scrooge.	True	False
8.	The ghost leads Scrooge by the hand through his bedroom window.	True	False

Track 10

B. Read and listen to Chapter Two, pp. 49–53. Then, fill in the blanks in the statements below.

1. First, the Ghost of Christmas Past brings Scrooge to the place where he ________________.
2. Next, they go to a ________________, where they see some people riding a wagon.
3. Then, Scrooge sees himself as a boy, sitting ________________.
4. When Scrooge sees himself, he ________________.
5. Scrooge remembers how he used to imagine the characters from ________________.
6. Suddenly, Scrooge remembers the boy who was ________________, and he feels sorry that he didn't ________________.

Track 11

C. Read Chapter Two, pp. 54–61, and listen. Then fill in the chart below.

Character	Description/Action	How Scrooge Feels About Him/Her
Fan	*Scrooge's sister ...*	
Mr. Fezziwig		
Dick Wilkins		

Tracks 9–11

D. Reread Chapter Two, pp. 42–61, as you listen to the audio again. Then match the vocabulary words below with their definitions.

1. ______ cap		**a.**	units of money in Britain
2. ______ well-being		**b.**	to know someone or something from seeing them before
3. ______ blindfolded		**c.**	a vehicle pulled by horses
4. ______ recognize		**d.**	health and happiness
5. ______ carol		**e.**	a cover
6. ______ parlor		**f.**	room used for receiving guests
7. ______ carriage		**g.**	should have something
8. ______ pounds		**h.**	unable to see because of a cloth covering the eyes
9. ______ deserve		**i.**	a Christmas song
10. ______ praise		**j.**	something that gives pleasure
11. ______ enjoyable		**k.**	approval

Teacher's Notes

Worksheet 10

This worksheet covers the remaining part of Chapter Two, pp. 61–68.

Track 12

A. Starting at the third row on p. 61, have students read to the first row on p. 65. Play the audio as they read. Ask them to circle the name of the person who says each of the quotes.

ANSWER KEY: 1. Belle; **2.** Scrooge; **3.** Scrooge; **4.** Belle; **5.** Scrooge; **6.** Belle

Track 13

B. Starting at the second row on p. 65, have students read to p. 68. Play the audio as they read. Have students look for the answers to the questions as they read. Go over the answers as a class.

ANSWER KEY: 1. He saw Scrooge. **2.** He was sitting alone in his office. **3.** Jacob Marley is on his deathbed. This means that he is dying. **4.** He wants to go home. **5.** He puts the cap on the ghost and extinguishes its light.

Tracks 12–13

C. This activity reviews vocabulary words from this section. Have students complete the sentences with the correct words from the word bank.

ANSWER KEY: 1. relationship; **2.** measured; **3.** blamed; **4.** deathbed

Tracks 12–13

D. Have students reread and listen to Chapter Two, pp. 61–68. Then have students answer the questions in complete sentences.

SAMPLE ANSWERS: 1. Belle wants to end their relationship because Scrooge has changed. They used to be poor and happy together, but Scrooge only cares about money now. **2.** In the first scene, with Belle and Scrooge, the mood is very tense and very sad. Belle is crying, and Scrooge is unhappy. In the second scene, the mood is cheerful. Belle and her family smile and laugh when they talk about Scrooge.

Discussion questions:

- Compare the scenes from Scrooge's youth (pp. 42–61) to the scenes with Belle (pp. 61–68). How has Scrooge changed from when he was young to when he was with Belle? (Sample answer: Scrooge used to have relationships with people. He used to love his sister. He had friends and enjoyed Christmas. But in the later scenes, Belle says that he loves money more than anything else. He doesn't care about people anymore.)
- Think about how Scrooge's character has changed over time. How did Scrooge become who he is today? What factors in his life contributed to him becoming a coldhearted miser? (Sample answer: Scrooge was often alone when he was a child. It seems like his father was not kind to him. He was away from his family when he went to school. Scrooge was poor until he was older. He probably wanted to make a lot of money so he wouldn't be poor ever again. But Belle ended their relationship because he loved money too much. So, Scrooge was alone again. This probably made him very sad. He probably decided to stay alone and to concentrate on his business. Human relationships were a disappointment to Scrooge, but making money was something he could always do, and he was good at it.)

Name: ______________________________

While You Read

Worksheet 10 – Chapter Two: The First Ghost, pp. 61–68

Track 12

A. Read Chapter Two, pp. 61–65, as you listen. Decide who said each quote below. Circle your answer.

1.	"You care more about something else than you do about me."	Scrooge	Belle
2.	"That's just the way the world is! It is hard on poor people."	Scrooge	Belle
3.	"But that doesn't change how I feel about you. Does it?"	Scrooge	Belle
4.	"You're a different person now."	Scrooge	Belle
5.	"I'm smarter now."	Scrooge	Belle
6.	"I hope you're happy with the life you've chosen!"	Scrooge	Belle

Track 13

B. Read Chapter Two, pp. 65–68. Listen to the audio as you read. Then answer the questions.

1. Who did Belle's husband see that day? ______________________________
2. Where did Belle's husband see him? ______________________________
3. Where is Marley? ____________________ What does this mean? ______________________________
4. What does Scrooge want to do after he sees this scene? ______________________________
5. What does he do to the Ghost of Christmas Past? ______________________________

Tracks 12–13

C. Complete each statement with the correct word from the word bank.

deathbed	measured	relationship	blamed

1. Scrooge used to have a ____________________ with a young woman named Belle.
2. Scrooge ____________________ the value of everything by how much money it would make.
3. Bell ____________________ Scrooge's love of money for the end of their love.
4. When Marley was sick and on his ____________________, Scrooge continued working in the office.

Tracks 12–13

D. Reread and listen to Chapter Two, pp. 61–68. Then answer the following questions.

1. Why does Belle want to end their relationship?

   ____

   ____

2. Compare the two scenes with Belle. How is the mood of the first scene different from the mood of the second scene?

   ____

   ____

Name: ____________________

Quiz 2

Worksheets 6–10

A. Read the clues below and fill in the correct words or names in the crossword puzzle.

Down

1. The girl Scrooge used to love
2. Marley's ghost must carry this
3. "Bah, ________!": What Scrooge says when he thinks something is nonsense.
4. A Christian religious song that is sung at Christmas
5. Scrooge's first name

Across

6. The Ghost of Christmas ________ shows Scrooge scenes from when he was a child
7. Bob Cratchit's job
8. Fred is Scrooge's ________
9. Scrooge's dead partner
10. An organization that raises money to help people in need
11. A mean person who is stingy with money
12. Scrooge's boss when he was young

B. Match the characters with their descriptions.

1.	________ Scrooge	a.	suffering; full of regret; must travel; has no rest and no peace
2.	________ Fred	b.	coldhearted; cares only about money; lives in his partner's house
3.	________ Bob	c.	happy but poor; works hard; has a large family
4.	________ Marley's ghost	d.	merry; friendly; invites his uncle to celebrate Christmas with him

C. Fill in the blanks to complete each statement.

1. At the beginning of the story, the only thing that Scrooge cares about is ________________.
2. Bob asks for ________________ off from work. Scrooge tells him to come in early the next day.
3. The first ghost to visit Scrooge is ________________.
4. Young Scrooge's ________________ comes to the school to take him home for Christmas.
5. Young Scrooge's boss, ________________, gives a big, enjoyable Christmas party at his office.

Name: ______________________________

Quiz 2 (Continued)
Worksheets 6–10

D. Look at the illustrations from the story. Write a sentence for each picture to describe what is happening.

1. 

____

____

2. 

____

____

3. 

____

____

4. 

____

____

Name: ____________________

Test 1

A. Circle the words that describe the elements of a novella. Cross out the words that are not elements of a novella.

theme	rhyme	conflict	characters	stage directions	mood
plot	facts	climax	diagrams	setting	photographs

Choose three of the elements you circled and write a definition for each element.

1. ____________________
2. ____________________
3. ____________________

B. Circle True or False. If the sentence is false, make it true and write it on the lines.

1. Dickens's father was very rich. True False
2. At the beginning of *A Christmas Carol*, Marley is still alive. True False
3. Scrooge agrees to let Bob take Christmas Day off from work. True False
4. Marley's ghost is cheerful and gives Scrooge good news. True False
5. The first place that the Ghost of Christmas Past takes Scrooge is to Mr. Fezziwig's office. True False
6. Scrooge once loved a girl named Belle, but he ended their relationship because she was poor. True False

Name: ______________________________

Test 1 (Continued)

C. Answer the following questions. Write 1–2 paragraphs.

1. Describe the Victorian era and the Industrial Revolution's effect on the lives of poor people in England. What evidence do you see of this in *A Christmas Carol: The Graphic Novel?*

2. Scrooge goes through many changes. How is the old miser Scrooge different from the young Scrooge? What changes do you see in Scrooge as a result of his experiences with the ghosts? Give evidence from the story.

Teacher's Notes
Worksheet 11

Track 14

A. Have students read Chapter Three, pp. 69–72, as they listen to the audio. Afterward, ask them to fill in the blanks without looking at their books. Then, have students check their answers.

Note: When students first see the image of the Ghost of Christmas Present on p. 71, point out the object he is holding in his left hand. It is a light source, but it is meant to look like a *cornucopia*, or "horn of plenty." Ask students if they recognize this symbol or know what it is. Explain that it is a symbol of *abundance* (a large quantity of something—in this case, food, wealth, happiness). It comes from Greek mythology. In one version of the story, the god Zeus, who as a child was raised on the milk of a female goat, accidentally breaks off one of the goat's horns. To make up for his mistake, he gives the horn special powers, so that it would be filled with whatever the owner wished for. Cornucopias are often shown as being filled with food (grains, fruits, etc.).

Discussion questions:

- How does the cornucopia symbol relate to Christmas? (The cornucopia is a symbol of abundance. It gives people whatever they wish for. Christmas is a time of abundance: big feasts, lots of gifts, and donating to poor people.)
- Who are the ghost's eighteen hundred older brothers? (All the ghosts of Christmas Present since the beginning of Christmas.)

ANSWER KEY: 1. one; **2.** Fifteen; **3.** Present; **4.** robe; **5.** 1,800/eighteen hundred; **6.** huge; **7.** lesson; **8.** touch

Note: The story assumes that Christmas has been celebrated since the establishment of Christianity in the first century; while there were some observances before it, Christmas was not established as an official Christian holiday on a fixed date until the fourth century, when the Roman emperor Constantine set it as December 25.

Track 15

B. Play the audio and have students read Chapter Three, pp. 73–76. Then, ask them to complete the questions independently, or go over them as a class.

SAMPLE ANSWERS: 1. to the streets of London; **2.** Christmas happiness; **3.** It helps poor people the most, because they need the most help. **4.** for closing the places where poor people can eat on Christmas Day; **5.** to Bob Cratchit's house

Track 16

C. This section covers Chapter Three, pp. 77–81. All of the statements here are false. Have students write true sentences on the line below each one.

ANSWER KEY: 1. Martha is Bob's daughter. **2.** Bob carries Tiny Tim through the front door. **3.** The Cratchits say a prayer before dinner. **4.** After dinner, everyone helps clean up. **5.** Tiny Tim says, "God bless us, every one!"

Tracks 14–16

D. This section reviews some of the vocabulary words from, Chapter Three, pp. 69–81. You may choose to do this activity first or as a section review.

ANSWER KEY: 1. d; **2.** a; **3.** b; **4.** e; **5.** c; **6.** f

Name: ______________________________

While You Read

Worksheet 11 – Chapter Three: The Second Ghost, pp. 69–81

Track 14

A. Listen to the audio as you read Chapter Three, pp. 69–72. Fill in the blanks in the summary below.

Scrooge and the Ghost of Christmas Present

Scrooge wakes up at 1. ______________ o'clock. 2. ______________ minutes pass before he hears the second ghost call him from the other room. Scrooge goes into the next room and sees the Ghost of Christmas 3. ______________. The ghost is very large and wears a long, green 4. ______________. The ghost tells Scrooge that he has more than 5. ______________ older brothers. Scrooge thinks that the ghost has a 6. ______________ family.

Scrooge tells the ghost that he learned an important 7. ______________ the night before, and he is sure he will learn something tonight. The ghost tells Scrooge to 8. ______________ his robe.

Track 15

B. Read Chapter Three, pp. 73–76, as you listen to the audio. Then answer the following questions.

1. Where does the Ghost of Christmas Present take Scrooge first? ______________
2. What does the Ghost of Christmas Present spread as he travels with Scrooge? ______________
3. Whom does it help the most? Why? ______________
4. What does Scrooge blame the Ghost of Christmas Present for? ______________
5. Where does the Ghost of Christmas Present take Scrooge next? ______________

Track 16

C. Read Chapter Three, pp. 77–81, and listen to the audio. Correct the following false statements.

1. Martha is Bob's servant.
____
2. Tiny Tim walks through the front door with Bob.
____
3. The Cratchits say a poem before dinner.
____
4. After dinner, the children play while Mrs. Cratchit cleans up.
____
5. Tiny Tim says, "God bless you!"
____

Tracks 14–16

D. Reread and listen to Chapter Three, pp. 69–81. Match the vocabulary words with their definitions.

1. ______ show off	a. very large
2. ______ huge	b. unable to walk
3. ______ lame	c. unable to see
4. ______ tremble	d. to display a skill proudly
5. ______ blind	e. to shake slightly
6. ______ lesson	f. an example from which you should learn

Teacher's Notes
Worksheet 12

Track 17

A. Play the audio as students read Chapter Three, pp. 82–84. They will find vocabulary words as they read. Students should understand most of the words in context. Have them match the words to the sentences, and go over them together as a class.

ANSWER KEY: 1. seat; **2.** crutch; **3.** embarrassed; **4.** complain; **5.** toast; **6.** feast; **7.** stingy; **8.** cast

Discussion questions:

- On p. 82, the Ghost of Christmas Present repeats something Scrooge said earlier, back at Scrooge. What does the ghost say? ("If he's going to die, shouldn't he just hurry up and do it?")
- When did Scrooge say that? (In Chapter One, p. 19, to the charity collectors.)
- Why is Scrooge embarrassed that the Ghost of Christmas Present repeats it? (His attitude has changed. He is starting to care about people again.)

Track 18

B. Have students read Chapter Three, pp. 85–88, as you play the audio. Stop reading at the first row on p. 88.

Note: Point out lighthouse on p. 87. Explain that *lighthouse* is a compound word, and ask students to break it down (*light* + *house*). Ask students if they have seen one before, and if they know or can guess what it is for. (It's a tower built near or in the sea, with a lamp to guide ships.)

Have students read the descriptions of the places the Ghost of Christmas Present takes Scrooge. Students should write the letters a.–e. in the order in which Scrooge and the ghost visit them.

ANSWER KEY: 1. b; **2.** e; **3.** a; **4.** d; **5.** c

Track 19

C. Beginning with the second row on p. 88, have students read to p. 91 as you play the audio. As they read, tell them to look for the ways in which Christmas at Fred's is similar to and different from Christmas at Bob's.

SAMPLE ANSWERS:
Similarities: Both families have a feast. Both Fred and Bob make a toast to Scrooge. Something negative is said about Scrooge. Both celebrations have an effect on Scrooge.

Differences: Fred is not as poor as Bob. Fred has a big party, and there are only adults. Only Bob's wife and children are present at his dinner. At Fred's party they play games. At Fred's house, they can laugh about Scrooge, but Scrooge's name casts a shadow over the party at Bob's house.

Track 20

D. Have the students read Chapter Three, pp. 92–95. Stop reading at the first row on p. 95.

Review the meaning of *ignorance* (not knowing something) and *want* (extreme poverty). Point out the relationship of the noun *want* to the verb to *want*. When we want something, we don't have it, but we feel a desire or need for it. Another, generally older meaning of to *want* is simply to need something that you don't have.
Have students answer the comprehension questions independently or as a class.

SAMPLE ANSWERS: 1. At midnight. He is the Ghost of Christmas Present, so he only exists in the present moment, on Christmas. **2.** They symbolize ignorance and want. These are dangerous problems that people face all around the world.

Name: ______________________________

While You Read

Worksheet 12 – Chapter Three: The Second Ghost, pp. 82–95

Track 17

A. Read Chapter Three, pp. 82–84, as you listen to the audio. Fill in the blanks with words from the word bank.

embarrassed	cast	crutch	complain	seat	stingy	toast	feast

1. The ghost sees an empty ______________ at the table where Tiny Tim used to sit.
2. Tiny Tim uses a ______________ to help him walk.
3. Scrooge is ______________ by the way he used to speak about poor people.
4. Scrooge used to ______________ about poor people. He didn't think they deserved his help.
5. After dinner, Bob raises his glass in a ______________ to honor Mr. Scrooge.
6. A ______________ is a large dinner for a celebration.
7. A miser, like Scrooge, is a ______________ person.
8. Where there is light, a person or a thing will ______________ a shadow.

Track 18

B. Read Chapter Three, pp. 85–88, as you listen to the audio. The Ghost of Christmas Present leads Scrooge to several places after they leave the Cratchits' house. Put the places in the order that Scrooge and the Ghost of Christmas Present visit them.

1. ______ a. a lighthouse
2. ______ b. the streets
3. ______ c. Fred's house
4. ______ d. a ship at sea
5. ______ e. where the coal miners live

Track 19

C. Now read Chapter Three, pp. 88–91, as you listen to the audio. Compare and contrast Christmas at Fred's house to Christmas at Bob's house. List the similarities and differences below.

Similarities:

____

____

____

Differences:

____

____

____

Track 20

D. Read Chapter Three, pp. 92–95, as you listen to the audio. Answer the questions.

1. When will the Ghost of Christmas Present's life end? Why?

____

____

2. What do the two children on p. 94 symbolize? Why does the Ghost of Christmas Present say that they belong to humankind?

____

____

____

Teacher's Notes
Worksheet 13

Track 21

A. Play the audio and have students read Chapter Four, pp. 95–99. Then ask them to answer the questions.

ANSWER KEY: 1. The Ghost of Christmas to Come wears a long, black robe with a hood. His face isn't showing. Only his hands are showing. They look like claws or skeleton hands. He does not speak; he only points. He is more mysterious and scarier than the Ghost of Christmas Present. The Ghost of Christmas Present was very merry and went around spreading Christmas happiness. **2.** The mood of this chapter is dark and scary. Chapter Three was merry because it showed happy people celebrating Christmas. **3.** They are talking about a rich man who just died. They are probably talking about Scrooge.

Discussion questions:

- Who or what does the Ghost of Christmas to Come remind you of? (Answers will vary, but many will say "Death," since this is how Death is commonly portrayed. Another name in English you might want to share with students is "The Grim Reaper.")
- What do you imagine the ghost's face might look like? (Answers will vary. Some students will say "skull" or "skeleton.")

Track 22

B. Play the audio while students read Chapter Four, pp. 100–107. Have students read the statements and circle the correct word to complete each one.

ANSWER KEY: 1. poor; **2.** shop; used; **3.** Three; **4.** stole; dead; **5.** curtains; blankets; **6.** shirt; body

Discussion questions:

- How were these three people able to steal all of these things, including the shirt off the man's back? (The man died alone and had no one to take care of him, so there probably wasn't anyone around to stop them.)
- The cleaning woman says several things to justify their actions. Find at least three examples of this in the graphic novel. (p. 102: "Everyone has a right to take care of themselves—he always did." "He won't miss these things. He's dead." p. 103: "We just helped ourselves to this stuff. It isn't a sin." p. 106: "And I don't feel bad about it." "Well, he doesn't need them.")

Track 23

C. Play the audio as students read Chapter Four, pp. 108–113. Have them decide whether each statement is True or False. As a follow-up, ask students to correct the false statements orally as a class.

ANSWER KEY: 1. True; **2.** False. He is too afraid to look. **3.** True; **4.** False. The family is happy. **5.** True

Tracks 21–23

D. This is a review of the vocabulary from this section. Have students complete the paragraph with the correct words.

ANSWER KEY: 1. met his maker; **2.** contagious; **3.** take care of; **4.** buried; **5.** broke; **6.** trivial

Name: ______________________________

While You Read

Worksheet 13 – Chapter Four: The Last Ghost, pp. 95–113

Track 21

A. Listen to and read Chapter Four, pp. 95–99. Then answer the questions.

1. Describe the Ghost of Christmas to Come. How is he different from the Ghost of Christmas Present?

____

____

2. How is the **mood** of this chapter different from the mood of Chapter Three?

____

____

3. What are the mens' conversations about on pp. 97–99? Whom do you think they are talking about?

____

____

Track 22

B. Listen to and read Chapter Four, pp. 100–107. Circle the correct words to complete the sentences.

1. The ghost takes Scrooge to a **rich / poor** part of town.

2. Old Joe is the owner of a **shop / school** that sells **used / new** things.

3. **Two / Three** people arrive at the store with some items to sell.

4. They **bought / stole** the items from a **dead / sick** man.

5. The cleaning woman brings the man's **curtains / boots** and **books / blankets**.

6. She even took the man's best **shirt / robe** from his **body / closet**!

Track 23

C. Listen to and read Chapter Four, pp. 108–113. Decide if the statements are True or False. Circle your answer.

1. The ghost shows Scrooge a dead person lying under a sheet.	True	False
2. Scrooge looks under the sheet to see the face of the person.	True	False
3. Scrooge asks to see someone who feels something about the man's death.	True	False
4. The ghost shows him a family who is sad about the man's death.	True	False
5. The family owed money to the dead man.	True	False

Tracks 21–23

D. Reread and listen to Chapter Four, pp. 95–113. Complete the paragraph with the words from the word bank.

take care of	buried	met his maker	trivial	contagious	broke

Trivial Conversations

The old man finally 1. ______________. He didn't die of a 2. ______________ disease. He died alone, with no one to 3. ______________ him. They 4. ______________ him in the churchyard, but no one came to the funeral. He wasn't 5. ______________ when he died, but all his money could not help him in the end. This is not a 6. ______________ story; there is an important lesson to learn here.

Teacher's Notes
Worksheet 14

Track 24

A. Play the audio and have students follow along on Chapter Four, pp. 114–117. Then ask students to circle True or False. As a follow-up exercise, go over the statements with the class and ask them to correct the false statements orally.

ANSWER KEY: 1. False. Scrooge recognizes them but can't remember exactly where he heard them. **2.** False. Bob used to walk faster with Tiny Tim on his shoulders. Now he walks more slowly. **3.** True; **4.** False. Bob promised Tiny Tim that he would visit the graveyard every Sunday.

Note: Point out the first row on p. 114. Explain that the line Peter is reading ("And He took a child, and set him among them . . .") is from the Christian Bible. Scrooge recognizes the words because he probably used to go to church when he was younger, but stopped when money became the focus of his life. In Victorian England, going to church and reading the Bible were considered good and virtuous activities.

Track 25

B. Play the audio for Chapter Four, pp. 118–120, and have students follow along in their books. Have students answer the questions independently or go over them together as a class.

SAMPLE ANSWERS: 1. Scrooge's nephew, Fred; **2.** Yes. Fred was kind and expressed sadness over Tiny Tim's death. He offered to help the Cratchits. **3.** Fred might get Peter a good job. **4.** Bob wants his children to remember Tiny Tim, try to be as good as he was, and not get into arguments easily.

Track 26

C. This section covers the last part of Chapter Four and also reviews vocabulary from this and other sections of the graphic novel. Have students listen to the audio as they read Chapter Four, pp. 121–126. Then have them complete the summary using vocabulary words from the word bank.

ANSWER KEY: 1. countinghouse; **2.** headstone; **3.** dismayed; **4.** lesson; **5.** applies; **6.** softened; **7.** celebrate; **8.** make up for; **9.** avoid

Discussion question: Can you predict what will happen next? Do you think Scrooge will get a second chance? Will he act differently? (Answers will vary. Yes, Scrooge will probably get a second chance. He will be more kind and generous.)

Name: ____________________

While You Read

Worksheet 14 – Chapter Four: The Last Ghost, pp. 114–126

Track 24

A. Read and listen to Chapter Four, pp. 114–117. Decide if the statements are True or False. Circle your answer.

1. Scrooge doesn't recognize the words that the boy is reading.	True	False
2. Bob walks faster now without Tiny Tim on his shoulders.	True	False
3. Tiny Tim is dead.	True	False
4. Bob promised Tiny Tim that he would visit the graveyard every day.	True	False

Track 25

B. Listen to and read Chapter Four, pp. 118–120. Then answer the questions.

1. Who did Bob see while he was out?

____

2. Was it a pleasant meeting? Why?

____

____

3. Why is Peter happy?

____

____

4. What does Bob ask his children to do?

____

____

Track 26

C. Read and listen to Chapter Four, pp. 121–126. Then fill in the blanks in the summary using words from the word bank.

applies	headstone	make up for	dismayed	celebrate
avoid	lesson	softened	countinghouse	

Learning a Lesson

Scrooge wants to know the identity of the dead man they saw. The Ghost of Christmas to Come takes Scrooge near the 1. ____________ where he works. Scrooge sees someone in his office. Then, the Ghost of Christmas to Come takes him to the churchyard and points to a 2. ____________. Scrooge is 3. ____________ to see his own name on the grave.

Scrooge tells the Ghost of Christmas to Come that he has learned his 4. ____________: "If we change how we act, then we change our lives, too." He asks the ghost if this 5. ____________ to his situation. Scrooge promises that he has changed. His heart has 6. ____________. He will 7. ____________ Christmas and 8. ____________ all of his cruel and stingy behavior in the past. He begs the Ghost of Christmas to Come to tell him that he can 9. ____________ this miserable future. But, the ghost says nothing. Then, suddenly, Scrooge is alone, back in his bedroom.

Teacher's Notes

Worksheet 15

Track 27

A. Play the audio as the students read Chapter Five, pp. 127–132. Have students read the sentences and choose the word or words that correctly complete each sentence.

ANSWER KEY: 1. b; **2.** a; **3.** c; **4.** a; **5.** b; **6.** b

Discussion question: Why does Scrooge stop to look at his door knocker? Why does he call it wonderful and say he will love it as long as he lives? (In Chapter One, p. 24, Scrooge thinks he sees Marley's face in the door knocker. That was the beginning of the big adventure that changed his life.)

Track 28

B. Play the audio as students read Chapter Five, pp. 133–136. Have students put the events in the order they happened in the story.

ANSWER KEY: 1. f; **2.** b; **3.** e; **4.** d; **5.** g; **6.** a; **7.** c

Track 29

C. Play the audio as the students read Chapter Five, pp. 137–140. Have students answer the questions.

SAMPLE ANSWERS: 1. Scrooge acts like his old self and pretends that he is angry with Bob for being late. But then Scrooge surprises Bob by saying that he is going to give Bob a raise. **2.** Tiny Tim doesn't die. Scrooge becomes like a second father to him. **3.** Scrooge was happy to see them laughing. **4.** Scrooge loves Christmas now. He becomes known for celebrating Christmas better than anyone else.

Discussion question: In the future that the Ghost of Christmas to Come shows Scrooge, Tiny Tim dies. But because Scrooge changes his own future by changing his behavior, Tiny Tim lives. Explain why Scrooge's actions change the future of the child. Why would Tiny Tim die if Scrooge didn't change? (Sample answer: Bob's family is very poor. Maybe they could not afford medical treatment for him. Maybe they couldn't buy enough food and coal to keep him healthy and warm—this would especially be true if Scrooge were to die and leave Bob jobless. Perhaps when Scrooge becomes kind and generous, gives Bob more money, and takes special care of Tiny Tim, Tiny Tim is able to see a doctor. Then, he grows strong and healthy.)

D. This is a review of vocabulary words in the section. One word is new. Ask the students to complete the definitions of the words without looking them up in the glossary. Have them try to figure out the meaning from the context in the story. After they write the definitions, they can check the glossary, or you can go over the answers as a class.

SAMPLE ANSWERS: 1. that the worker will get paid more money; **2.** he or she is having a difficult time; **3.** something on a door that helps you knock on it; **4.** say nice things about them

Name: ____________________

While You Read

Worksheet 15 – Chapter Five: The End, pp. 127–140

Track 27

A. Listen to and read Chapter Five, pp. 127–132. Circle the letter of the correct answer.

1. When Scrooge discovers he is back in his room, he ________ God and Christmastime
   a. toasts   b. praises   c. regrets
2. He goes to the living room and points to ________ places where he saw ghosts.
   a. three   b. four   c. two
3. He goes to the window and asks a boy ________.
   a. what his name is   b. what time it is   c. what day it is
4. He sends the boy to buy a ________.
   a. turkey   b. cake   c. basket of fruit
5. The turkey is for ________.
   a. Fred   b. Bob   c. himself
6. As Scrooge waits for the boy to return, he looks at his door ________ and says he will love it as long as he lives.
   a. knob   b. knocker   c. bell

Track 28

B. Listen to and read Chapter Five, pp. 133–136. Put the following events in order.

1. ______	a. Scrooge visits his nephew, Fred.
2. ______	b. He puts on his best clothes.
3. ______	c. He dances and enjoys the Christmas party.
4. ______	d. Scrooge goes to church.
5. ______	e. He apologizes and offers money to the charity collectors.
6. ______	f. Scrooge sits in his house and laughs until he cries.
7. ______	g. Scrooge walks with people in the streets.

Track 29

C. Read and listen to Chapter Five, pp. 137–140. Then answer the questions.

1. What joke does Scrooge play on Bob the day after Christmas?

____

____

2. What happens to Tiny Tim?

____

____

3. How does Scrooge react when people laugh at his changed personality?

____

____

4. How has Scrooge's attitude toward Christmas changed?

____

____

Tracks 27–29

D. Give a brief explanation of each underlined vocabulary word, in your own words.

1. If a boss gives a worker a <u>raise</u>, it means ________________________.
2. If someone is <u>struggling</u>, it means ________________________.
3. A <u>door knocker</u> is ________________________.
4. If you <u>praise</u> someone, you ________________________.

Name: ______________________________

Quiz 3
Worksheets 11–15

A. Match the quote with the character who said it.

1. ______ "God bless us, every one!"
2. ______ "Some people on earth do bad things in our name. Remember that, and don't blame us!"
3. ______ "I will live in the past, present, and future!"
4. ______ "Only on Christmas Day would we toast such a stingy person as Mr. Scrooge."
5. ______ "He scared everyone when he was alive, now we can make money from his death!"
6. ______ "When we think about how good he was, we will try to behave the same way he did, and we won't get into arguments very easily."

a. Ghost of Christmas Present
b. Cleaning woman
c. Bob
d. Tiny Tim
e. Scrooge
f. Mrs. Cratchit

B. Put the following events from the story in order.

1. ______
2. ______
3. ______
4. ______
5. ______
6. ______

a. The Ghost of Christmas Present takes Scrooge to Fred's house.
b. Scrooge goes to Fred's house for Christmas dinner.
c. Scrooge becomes a second father to Tiny Tim.
d. The Ghost of Christmas to Come takes Scrooge to the Cratchits' home.
e. The Ghost of Christmas Present takes Scrooge to the Cratchits' home.
f. The Ghost of Christmas to Come shows Scrooge his headstone.

C. Write a brief description of each character and their role in the story.

1. The Ghost of Christmas Present: ______________________________
2. The Ghost of Christmas to Come: ______________________________
3. Old Joe: ______________________________
4. Tiny Tim: ______________________________

Teacher's Notes

Worksheet 16

This worksheet revisits some of the vocabulary words from *A Christmas Carol: The Graphic Novel* while reviewing the key characters.

A. Ask students to look at the word bank. Have them apply the appropriate adjectives to the characters in the boxes. They don't need to use all of the adjectives, but encourage them to try. Tell them that they can use each adjective more than once.

Note: Not all of the adjectives are vocabulary words from the story. Have students look up the unknown words in a dictionary. They can probably guess the meanings of *warmhearted* and *selfless*. As an expansion, have students add adjectives of their own or find additional adjectives in a thesaurus.

SAMPLE ANSWERS: Scrooge: (before) rich, stingy, coldhearted, foolish, threatening, intimidating, mean, miserable, selfish; **(after)** merry, generous, kind, warmhearted, happy, selfless

Tiny Tim: merry, poor, lame, patient, warmhearted, loving, happy, selfless, gentle

Fred: merry, generous, kind, patient, warmhearted, loving, loyal, happy

The Ghost of Christmas Present: merry, generous, kind, warmhearted, helpful, wise, happy, selfless

Bob: poor, kind, patient, warmhearted, loving, loyal, selfless, gentle

Marley's Ghost: scary, helpful, miserable

The Ghost of Christmas Past: kind, scary, helpful, wise, gentle

The Ghost of Christmas to Come: scary, threatening, intimidating, wise, helpful

Optional activity: Have students choose one of the characters and find evidence in the book that supports the adjectives they chose. For example, Scrooge is **stingy** and **selfish** because he refuses to give money to poor people in Chapter One, pp. 16–19.

Discussion question: How does each character help move the story along and develop the plot? What role does each one play in the story? (**Scrooge:** The main character; we see everything through his eyes. **Fred:** Scrooge's only relative. His personality contrasts with Scrooge's. He seems to reflect the narrator's opinions and way of thinking. Through him we see everything that's wrong with Scrooge's way of thinking. **Tiny Tim:** His innocence, his disability, his kindness, and his poverty combine to make him a very sympathetic character. We, along with Scrooge, start to care what happens to Tiny Tim. **The Ghost of Christmas Present:** He allows Scrooge to see how the people around him live, what they think of him, and how his actions affect them. **Bob Cratchit:** He represents the suffering worker of the Victorian era. Scrooge's cruelty and selfishness is highlighted when contrasted to Bob's gentle, loyal, kind personality. Scrooge does not know or understand Bob until the ghosts show him Bob's home life. **Marley's Ghost:** He is the first ghost that Scrooge meets, and his warnings to Scrooge mark the beginning of Scrooge's transformation. **The Ghost of Christmas Past:** Scrooge starts to soften when he sees the scenes from his own past. **The Ghost of Christmas to Come:** This ghost probably has the deepest effect on Scrooge, as he shows him terrifying scenes from the future as it will be if Scrooge does not change. It is during this ghost's visit that we see the climax of the story and Scrooge's ultimate transformation.)

Name: ______________________________

After You Read

Worksheet 16 – Characters and Adjectives

A. Here are the characters from *A Christmas Carol: The Graphic Novel.* Which adjectives would you use to describe them? Fill in the boxes with adjectives from the word bank.

merry	generous	poor	rich
kind	scary	stingy	lame
patient	coldhearted	warmhearted	helpful
loving	intimidating	threatening	wise
foolish	loyal	mean	happy
miserable	selfish	selfless	gentle

Ebenezer Scrooge

Bob Cratchit

Tiny Tim Cratchit

Ghost of Jacob Marley

Fred

Ghost of Christmas Past

Ghost of Christmas

Ghost of Christmas to Come

Teacher's Notes
Worksheet 17

Many ghost stories are considered horror stories, and their purpose is to frighten the reader. The reader feels scared because the reader sympathizes with the main character. The reader doesn't want a ghost to harm them. Also, the ghosts don't usually help the main character, but rather scare them. Furthermore, ghost stories usually end badly for the main character.

Discussion questions:

- Does *A Christmas Carol* have a sympathetic main character? (No, we don't sympathize with Scrooge.)
- Does it have scary ghosts with bad intentions? (The ghosts come help Scrooge.)
- Does it have an unhappy ending? (The story ends well for Scrooge and the other characters.)
- Do you know any ghost or horror stories? What happens to the main character(s)? (Answers will vary)

A. Tell students that they will now prove that *A Christmas Carol* is a ghost story. Go over the other characteristics of a ghost story in the chart, and have them recall or look for evidence of each characteristic in *A Christmas Carol: The Graphic Novel.*

SAMPLE ANSWERS:

Ghosts: Marley's ghost and the traveling ghosts that accompany him, the Ghost of Christmas Past, the Ghost of Christmas Present, and the Ghost of Christmas to Come

Events that humans can't explain logically: Scrooge's door knocker changes into Marley's face; the ghosts can change size, fly, travel through walls, travel through time, etc.; three nights have supposedly passed, but Scrooge still wakes up on Christmas Day.

Darkness: The story begins at night; Marley's ghost visits Scrooge in his dark house; the scenes set in the future are especially dark; there is literal and metaphorical darkness throughout the story.

Spooky locations: The story starts in a churchyard, and the first page is a very spooky scene; Scrooge's dark, empty house is spooky, especially when he starts seeing strange things; the spookiest location is the graveyard at the end of Chapter Four with the Ghost of Christmas to Come.

Death: Marley died before the beginning of the story and visits Scrooge; in Scrooge's vision of the future, both he and Tiny Tim die.

Scary events: Scrooge is terrified of the ghosts, and especially by the scenes in the future. For us, the ghosts aren't very scary because we don't sympathize with Scrooge; however, we fear that Tiny Tim will die.

Revenge: The thieves in Chapter Four seem to be getting revenge on Scrooge by stealing from him when he's dead. A lot of the story shows Scrooge being "paid back" for his selfish actions.

A character's past catches up with them: Marley shows Scrooge that his past will catch up with him unless he changes. Scrooge is also forced to face the consequences of his actions as the three ghosts show him scenes from his past, present, and future.

"Good" characters become victims: Scrooge himself does not fit this category, but many of the characters are victims of poverty and of Scrooge's selfishness. The most notable is Tiny Tim.

Note: Explain to students that if something *catches up with you*, you are forced to deal with an unpleasant situation that you have been able to avoid until now. Explain that *revenge* involves hurting or punishing someone who has harmed you. To *pay someone back* is another way of saying "to get revenge on someone."

Name: ______________________________

After You Read

Worksheet 17 – Ghost Story?

A. Is *A Christmas Carol* a ghost story? It's different from many traditional ghost stories, and not everyone thinks of it as a ghost story. However, it has many of the elements of a ghost story. Complete the chart below with details from the story.

Elements of ghost stories	Evidence in *A Christmas Carol*
Ghosts	Marley's ghost ...
Events that humans can't explain logically	
Darkness	
Spooky locations	
Death	
Scary events	
Revenge	
A character's past catches up with them	
"Good" characters become victims	

Teacher's Notes
Worksheet 18

In this worksheet, students will debate topics relating to themes in *A Christmas Carol: The Graphic Novel* from Scrooge's two different points of view in the story.

A. Divide the class into two teams. Half of the class will represent the old, stingy Scrooge from the beginning of the story, and the other half will represent the new, redeemed Scrooge at the end of the story. (Alternately, you could have the second team represent Fred, Scrooge's nephew, as the old Scrooge's opponent.)

Ask students to read the debate topics and think about whether their character would agree or disagree with each statement.

ANSWER KEY: Old Scrooge: **1.** Agree; **2.** Agree; **3.** Agree; **4.** Disagree

New Scrooge or Fred: **1.** Disagree; **2.** Disagree; **3.** Disagree; **4.** Agree

B. Select one debate topic with students. Have each team work together to prepare arguments to support their position. Alternately, the students can be divided so that pairs or small groups are each working on each one of the debate topics. This way, you can stage individual student debates in front of the whole class.

Remind students that they must represent their character and his way of thinking, no matter what their own opinion is. Also remind them that they should try and anticipate their opponent's arguments. They should have a counter-argument ready for each of their opponent's likely arguments. Have them review the graphic novel to prepare.

C. Stage the debate and act as mediator. Allow each side to state their position on the topic and provide arguments. Allow each opposing side to respond to the arguments with counter-arguments. Give each side a chance to summarize and restate his/her argument at the end of the debate. Allow the class to vote on who won the debate based on how well he/she argued the topic. Ask them to base their vote not on their opinion of the topic, but on the quality and persuasiveness of the speakers' arguments.

If your class is very large, break it into groups, and assign student mediators to oversee individual debates. You can walk around and listen in, providing guidance and feedback to the groups as needed. Mediators can decide on the winners of the debates.

Name: ______________________________

After You Read

Worksheet 18 – Debate: New Scrooge vs. Old Scrooge

A. You are going to represent either the old, stingy Scrooge at the beginning of the story, or the cheerful, generous Scrooge at the end of the story. Read each of the debate topics below and decide whether your character agrees or disagrees.

My character: ______________________________

Debate topics:

1. Everyone should take care of him or herself. It is not society's responsibility to take care of poor people.	Agree	Disagree
2. Christmas is no different from any other day.	Agree	Disagree
3. People need money to be happy.	Agree	Disagree
4. Love and friendship are more important than money.	Agree	Disagree

B. Choose one debate topic and write your position on the topic. Support your position with arguments. Make sure you stay true to your character!

My position:	
Supporting arguments:	
Opponent's possible arguments:	**My counter-argument:**

C. Debate your topic with an opponent! Take notes on your opponent's arguments below.

____

____

____

____

Teacher's Notes
Worksheet 19

In this worksheet, students must match quotations from *A Christmas Carol: The Graphic Novel* with the characters who said them. The purpose is not to have students memorize lines from the story; rather, students should recognize elements of the characters' roles and personalities reflected in the words.

A. Have students cut out all 24 cards.

Method 1: Students work individually to match the quotes. Have a contest to see who can correctly match all 12 quotations the fastest. Alternately, students could work in pairs to match the quotes, and the fastest pair to match all the quotes wins.

Method 2: Use one set of cards per pair or small group. Put them all face down, and the students play "Concentration." Each student flips two cards. If the quote matches the speaker, the student keeps the pair. If not, the next student gets to flip a pair.

Expansion: After the quotes have been matched, call on students to explain the context of each quote. Where in the story is the quote from? What does the character mean, and what prompted him/her to say it?

ANSWER KEY:

Quote	Speaker
"Marley was dead... as dead as a doornail. There was no doubt about that." Chapter One, p. 7	The narrator
"The prisons and workhouses don't have enough money to keep poor people alive. We are raising money to buy them food and warm clothing." Chapter One, p. 18	Charity collector
"If I had my way, every idiot who says 'Merry Christmas' would be cooked in his own Christmas meal!" Chapter One, p. 13	Ebenezer Scrooge
"I'm sorry to see you like this—but I'll always celebrate Christmas." Chapter One, p. 15	Fred
"Tonight, I'm here to bring you a message. You still have a chance to avoid the suffering that I'm experiencing." Chapter One, p. 37	Marley's ghost
"These are the shadows of things that have already happened. They cannot see us." Chapter Two, p. 50	The Ghost of Christmas Past
"No more work tonight—it's Christmas Eve! Quick! Let's close the office!" Chapter Two, p. 57	Mr. Fezziwig
"You measure everything by how much money you can make. How could you be happy with a poor girl like me?" Chapter Two, p. 64	Belle
"Have you ever seen anything like me before?" Chapter Three, p. 71	The Ghost of Christmas Present
"A toast to Mr. Scrooge, who gave us this wonderful feast!" Chapter Three, p. 83	Bob
"If he were here, I'd tell him what I really think about him." Chapter Three, p. 84	Mrs. Cratchit
"Everyone has a right to take care of themselves—he always did." Chapter Four, p. 102	Cleaning woman

Name: ______________________________

After You Read

Worksheet 19 – Matching Quotes

A. Cut out all the cards and match the quote to the character who said it.

"Marley was dead ... as dead as a doornail. There was no doubt about that."	**Bob**
"The prisons and workhouses don't have enough money to keep poor people alive. We are raising money to buy them food and warm clothing."	**Belle**
"If I had my way, every idiot who says 'Merry Christmas' would be cooked in his own Christmas meal!"	**The narrator**
"I'm sorry to see you like this—but I'll always celebrate Christmas."	**Cleaning woman**
"Tonight, I'm here to bring you a message. You still have a chance to avoid the suffering that I'm experiencing."	**The Ghost of Christmas Present**
"These are the shadows of things that have already happened. They cannot see us."	**Scrooge**

Name: ____________________

Worksheet 19 – Matching Quotes (continued)

"No more work tonight—it's Christmas Eve! Quick! Let's close the office!"	**Mrs. Cratchit**
"You measure everything by how much money you can make. How could you be happy with a poor girl like me?"	**Marley's ghost**
"Have you ever seen anything like me before?"	**Mr. Fezziwig**
"A toast to Mr. Scrooge, who gave us this wonderful feast!"	**The Ghost of Christmas Past**
"If he were here, I'd tell him what I really think about him."	**Charity collector**
"Everyone has a right to take care of themselves—he always did."	**Fred**

Teacher's Notes
Worksheet 20

The purpose of this worksheet is for students to use their creativity while reviewing, analyzing, and summarizing Scrooge's life and character.

A. Explain that an *obituary* is an account of a person's life and achievements that is published soon after they die. Read the sample obituary with students. Ask them to point out what information is included in the obituary. (The woman's name, nickname, age, occupation, town of residence, description of personality, manner of death, day of death, living relatives.)

If you have a newspaper handy, locate the obituary section and photocopy part of it to distribute to students as an additional example.

Tell students they are going to write an obituary for Scrooge. They can either write one for Scrooge as he was at the end of A *Christmas Carol*, or they can write the obituary for Scrooge as he was in the future vision shown by the Ghost of Christmas to Come—Scrooge as he would be if he did not change his ways. Alternately, you could have students write *both* versions of the obituary.

Discussion questions:

- What would the obituary of a stingy person who had no friends include? (It would probably be short and include only basic information.)
- What would the obituary of a generous person who was loved by many people in the community include? (It would probably be long and have a lot of kind details about the person.)

B. The students' first step is to figure out what information they need to include based on the sample obituary. Then they'll need to look for the relevant information about Scrooge in the graphic novel. If they can't find the information (e.g., his date of birth, date of death, manner of death), students can use their reasoning skills and imagination. For example, we don't know what year Scrooge was born in, but we can imagine that in the story he might be between 60 and 70 years old. The story was published in 1843, so if we assume that the story also takes place in that year, Scrooge would have been born between 1773 and 1783. Ask students what they think Scrooge's profession was. It is never explicitly mentioned. Possible answers include moneylender, banker, property owner, or investor.

ANSWER KEY: 1. full name: Ebenezer Scrooge; **2.** occupation: answers will vary; **3.** cause of death: answers will vary; **4.** date of death: answers will vary; **5.** age: answers will vary; **6.** description of personality: answers will vary; **7.** town of residence: London; **8.** living relatives: Fred, his nephew

C. Have the students write Scrooge's obituary. Encourage students to add details and description, particularly to the obituary of the kind and generous Scrooge.

Note: The sample obituary supplied is very basic. Students can write a more detailed obituary for Scrooge if they wish.

Name: ______________________________

After You Read

Worksheet 20 – Scrooge's Obituary

A. Look at the sample obituary.

Madeline Walsh, beloved Portsmouth librarian for more than 40 years, died Sunday night of heart failure. She was 90. Madeline, known as "Mimi," was known and loved by the entire community for her friendly personality and her volunteer work. She leaves behind two children, Pete and Elizabeth, six grandchildren, four great-grandchildren, and a younger brother, Thomas.

B. What information does an obituary include? Complete the chart below. In the left column, write the different kinds of information in an obituary. In the right column, write Scrooge's information. Look for the information in *A Christmas Carol: The Graphic Novel*, and use your imagination to fill in the missing details.

Information in an obituary	Information about Scrooge
1. full name	Ebenezer Scrooge
2.	
3.	
4.	
5.	

C. Now, write an obituary for Scrooge. Use the information from your chart, and add details of your own.

Teacher's Notes

Optional Worksheet

This is a fun worksheet in which students write and perform original deleted scenes from *A Christmas Carol: The Graphic Novel*.

A. Put the students into small groups (2–4 students per group) and assign a scenario from p. 54 to each group, or have them choose one. Alternately, a group may have their own original idea for a deleted scene (perhaps a scene from Scrooge's childhood, showing his relationship with his father; or a scene with Scrooge and his sister, after she has her child or when she is dying).
Ask students to make notes about the characters in the chart. This will prepare them to write scripts in which the characters behave consistently with the way they behave in the graphic novel. Refer students back to Worksheet 16 – Characters and Adjectives for ideas.

B. Explain to students that a *screenplay* is a script, or the words to be spoken in a movie or television program. It also includes the instructions about what will be seen in it. Point out the format and the different parts of the sample screenplay.

- The setting
  - EXT. is short for "exterior." This is for scenes that take place outside.
  - INT. is short for "interior." This is used for any scene that takes place inside a building.
  - Right after EXT. or INT. the student should write where the scene takes place (street, Bob Cratchit's house, Scrooge's office, etc.).
  - After the location, the student should include the time of day (morning, day, evening, night). If the day itself is significant (i.e., Christmas Day), include it.
- Action lines
  - Action lines tell what the characters are doing. Action lines should appear between dialogue whenever needed.
- Dialogue
  - Dialogue should be centered, with the character's name in all caps.
  - Dialogue sound natural, like real speech, and should match the style used in the graphic novel. This story takes place in the nineteenth century, so there shouldn't be any modern slang or references to later inventions or historical events.
  - The first time a character appears, their name should be in all caps. Include a physical description of the character.
- Parentheticals
  - Parentheticals convey how a character delivers a line, or small actions, such as a smile or hand movement.
  - These are just one or two words in parentheses under the character's name in the dialogue.

Note: Students can use a narrator if that will help them set up the scene. The narrator would have lines but would not appear on screen. Include "V.O." in parentheses next to NARRATOR in the dialogue, to indicate that the line is a voiceover.

C. Have students rehearse their scenes several times before performing them. Help students with pronunciation, intonation, and expression.
A fun way to enhance this activity would be to bring in a video camera and record the scenes. Replay them on a computer or TV screen for students to watch.

Name: ______________________________

After You Read

Optional Worksheet – Deleted Scenes

Imagine you have just watched a movie adaptation of A *Christmas Carol: The Graphic Novel* on DVD. Now, you click on the "Special Features" in the DVD menu to see the deleted scenes. These are scenes that the director originally wanted to include but had to cut because the movie was too long.

A. Choose one of the scenarios from the next page. In the chart below, make notes about the characters in the scene. Include who will play each character, what type of clothes they should wear, and how the character should act. Think about their personality, emotions, and behavior in the story.

Character	Actor	Clothing	Personality/Emotions

B. Now, write your scene in the form of a screenplay. Include the setting, the dialogue, and the actions of the characters. Here is an example:

```
EXT. street, day.
EBENEZER SCROOGE walks happily down the street. He tips his hat and
smiles at people he passes. Suddenly, he sees BELLE approaching.

                         SCROOGE
                        (excited)
                 Belle? Belle? Is that you?

Scrooge removes his hat and smiles a huge, laughing smile.

                          BELLE
                        (confused)
          Yes... that is my name. Do I know you, sir?

                         SCROOGE
                  Belle, it's me, Ebenezer!

Belle stares closely at his face and suddenly recognizes him.

                          BELLE
     Ebenezer Scrooge? I can't believe it! You are so changed!

                         SCROOGE
     I am more changed than you know, my dear. I am a new man!
```

C. Now, prepare to perform your scene in front of the class. Remember your character's personality and the mood of the scene.

Name: ______________________________

After You Read

Optional Worksheet – Deleted Scenes (continued)

Scenario 1
Parts: 4

The four ghosts—Marley and the Ghost of Christmas Past, the Ghost of Christmas Present, and the Ghost of Christmas to Come—get together on Christmas to discuss their experiences with Scrooge.

(Remember, the Ghost of Christmas to Come doesn't speak, so find other ways for him to communicate. This could be a funny scene!)

Scenario 2
Parts: 2 minimum

It's the day after Christmas, and Scrooge is walking down the street. He unexpectedly meets Belle, the woman he used to love.

They have a conversation.

(This scenario is full of dramatic possibility. Perhaps Belle is now a widow!)

Scenario 3
Parts: 3 minimum

The Cratchit family receive their Christmas turkey, delivered by the boy Scrooge paid

They try to figure out who sent it.

(You can add Cratchit children, depending on how many are in your group.)

Scenario 4
Parts: 2 or 3

It's Christmas Eve, and Bob meets Fred in the street on his way home from the office.

They talk about Christmas and about Scrooge.

(If you want to add parts, the two men could run into an old business associate of Scrooge's, like Dick Wilkins. Dick could walk by and overhear Scrooge's name.)

Scenario 5
Parts: 2 minimum

The two charity collectors leave Scrooge's office after Scrooge has refused to give them a donation.

They discuss Scrooge's attitude and their charity work.

(Consider writing two short scenes: one after the men leave Scrooge's office, and one after they meet Scrooge on Christmas Day and he apologizes.)

Scenario 6
Parts: 2 minimum

It's Christmas Day, after Fred's dinner party.
Fred and his wife are discussing the party and the changes in Scrooge's behavior.
(If you want to add parts, add other guests from the party.)

Name: ____________________

Test 2

A. Complete the summary of the story using the words from the word bank.

generous	partner	nephew	miser	to Come	coldhearted
poor	die	Past	dead	celebrates	feast
donate	Christmas	suffer	clerk	Present	

Summary of A Christmas Carol

At the beginning of the story, Scrooge is a 1. ______________ 2. ______________ who hates 3. ______________. He refuses to 4. ______________ money to 5. ______________ people. And, he won't go to a Christmas 6. ______________ at his 7. ______________ Fred's house.

Things change when the ghost of his 8. ______________ 9. ______________, Jacob Marley, visits him. Marley warns Scrooge that if he doesn't change, he will 10. ______________ alone and miserable, and he will 11. ______________ forever.

Three more ghosts visit Scrooge. The first is the Ghost of Christmas 12. ______________. The second is the Ghost of Christmas 13. ______________, and the third is the Ghost of Christmas 14. ______________. They show Scrooge scenes that both move and frighten him.

In the end, Scrooge becomes a good and 15. ______________ man. He gives more money to his 16. ______________, Bob, and is kind to Bob's son, Tiny Tim. And Scrooge finally 17. ______________ Christmas!

B. Look at each of the illustrations. Write 1–2 sentences to summarize what is happening.

1

____
____
____

3

____
____
____

2

____
____
____

4

____
____
____

Name: ______________________________

Test 2 (continued)

C. Answer the following questions with 1–2 paragraphs.

1. What conditions and events in Scrooge's life cause him to become stingy and selfish? Give examples and evidence from the story.

2. What is the **conflict** in *A Christmas Carol: The Graphic Novel*? Describe the climax of the story. What is the main **theme**?

Quiz 1 and 2
Answer Keys

Quiz 1

A. **1.** f; **2.** c; **3.** e; **4.** a; **5.** g; **6.** b; **7.** d

B. **1.** *The Pickwick Papers*; **2.** Westminster Abbey; **3.** Victorian era; **4.** debt; **5.** poverty

C. **1.** setting; **2.** conflict; **3.** theme; **4.** plot; **5.** character; **6.** mood; **7.** climax

Quiz 2

A.

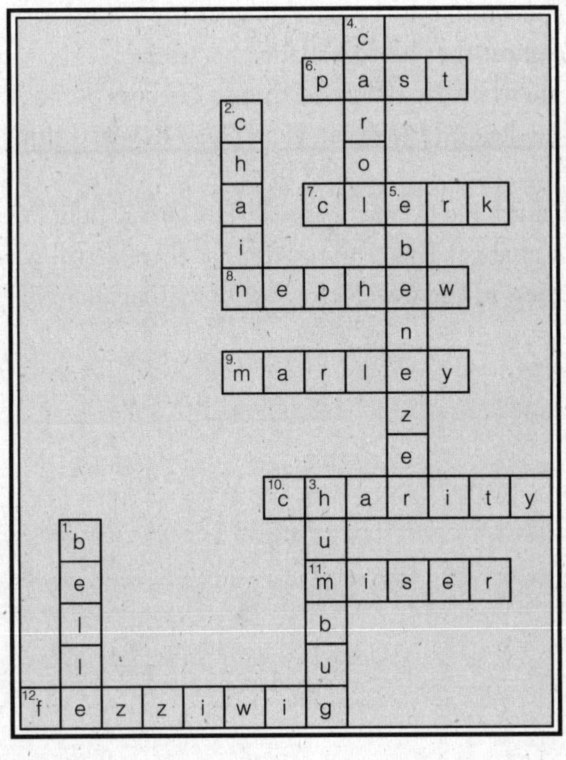

B. **1.** b; **2.** d; **3.** c; **4.** a

C. **1.** money/making money; **2.** Christmas Day; **3.** Marley; **4.** sister; **5.** Mr. Fezziwig

D.

1. Two men come to Scrooge's office looking for donations for the poor. Scrooge doesn't give them anything.
2. The ghost of Marley visits Scrooge and tells him about the suffering he is experiencing now because of the kind of life he lived.
3. The Ghost of Christmas Past takes Scrooge to the place where Scrooge grew up.
4. Belle tells Scrooge he has changed, and she doesn't want a relationship with him anymore. Scrooge tries to convince Belle that he is being smart—he doesn't want to be poor.

Quiz 3
Answer Key

A. **1.** d; **2.** a; **3.** e; **4.** f; **5.** b; **6.** c

B. **1.** e; **2.** a; **3.** d; **4.** f; **5.** b; **6.** c

C. SAMPLE ANSWERS:

1. The Ghost of Christmas Present wears a long green robe and is very merry. He spreads Christmas happiness everywhere he goes. He shows Scrooge what is happening in Scrooge's present Christmas. Most of the people who know Scrooge are suffering because of his actions.
2. The Ghost of Christmas to Come is scary. He wears a long black robe. He doesn't show his face, doesn't speak, and only points at things. He shows Scrooge what will happen in the future if Scrooge does not change. Scrooge finally sees that he is living his life the wrong way because of what the Ghost of Christmas to Come shows him. Scrooge promises the ghost that he will change his ways.
3. Old Joe is old, not rich, and dishonest. He owns a store where he sells used things. He buys Scrooge's things from three thieves who steal them after Scrooge dies. Old Joe is an example of how bad things can get when people live in poverty.
4. Tiny Tim is very small. He is happy, and a very good child. He is lame and sick. His father, Bob, loves him very much. Tiny Tim will die if Scrooge does not change. Tiny Tim proves that there is still good in people, even with all the evil, sickness, and selfishness in the world. He also shows that there is hope.

Test 1
Answer Key

A. Circled words: theme, conflict, characters, mood, plot, climax, setting
Crossed-out words: rhyme, stage directions, facts, diagrams, photographs
Students must include three of the following words and definitions.

SAMPLE ANSWERS:

theme: an important idea in a story
conflict: the main problem or struggle of the story
characters: people in the story
mood: the feeling or atmosphere of the story
plot: the events of a story
climax: the most exciting part of a story
setting: the time and place in which a story happens

B.

1. False. Dickens's father was not rich. He went to prison for debt.
2. False. At the beginning of *A Christmas Carol*, Jacob Marley, is dead/has been dead for seven years.
3. True
4. False. Marley's ghost is suffering and gives Scrooge bad news.
5. False. The first place that the Ghost of Christmas Past takes Scrooge is to the place where he grew up.
6. False. Scrooge once loved a girl named Belle, but she ended their relationship because he loved money more than he loved her.

C. SAMPLE ANSWERS:

1. The Victorian era was a time of change in England. The Industrial Revolution brought many people to the cities to work in factories, which created more wealth for rich people. But it was difficult for poor people. They lived and worked in very bad conditions.
   The Cratchit family is a good example of this. Bob has to work long hours, and he isn't paid very much. Bob has a large family and can't afford anything other than food for Christmas. Also, Bob's son Tiny Tim is very sick. Bob doesn't have enough money to pay for a doctor.
2. When Scrooge was young, he seemed happier. He had a sister he loved, a kind boss whom he liked, a friend named Dick Wilkins, and a girlfriend. He enjoyed Christmas. But the older Scrooge is coldhearted, has no friends, and only loves money. However, after he meets Marley's ghost and the Ghost of Christmas Past, he starts to change again. First, he is afraid of the suffering that Marley's ghost is experiencing. Then, he becomes emotional when he sees himself as a boy. Scrooge starts to remember the happiness he felt with his sister and at Fezziwig's party. Scrooge starts to regret his behavior.

Test 2
Answer Key

A. **1.** coldhearted; **2.** miser; **3.** Christmas; **4.** donate; **5.** poor; **6.** feast; **7.** nephew; **8.** dead; **9.** partner; **10.** die; **11.** suffer; **12.** Past; **13.** Present; **14.** to Come; **15.** generous; **16.** clerk **17.** celebrates

B. SAMPLE ANSWERS:

1. The Ghost of Christmas Present takes Scrooge out into the streets with him while he spreads Christmas happiness.
2. Scrooge sees his headstone and begs the Ghost of Christmas to Come to tell him that he can change his future.
3. Scrooge visits Fred on Christmas day. Everyone is surprised and happy to see him.
4. Scrooge pretends to be angry with Bob Cratchit, but then he surprises Bob. Scrooge tells Bob he is giving Bob a raise.

C. SAMPLE ANSWERS:

1. There were many reasons that Scrooge became a miser. When he was a child, his family was poor, and he knew that life was difficult for poor people. He focused on making money so that he would never be poor again. Also, he was alone a lot as a child and had to spend Christmas alone in his school. There is evidence in Chapter Two that his father was unkind to him. We also know that his sister died. All of these things make him sad and bitter. When he started focusing on money, he pushed away his girlfriend, Belle. Belle ended their relationship. This probably made Scrooge even more bitter, sad, and lonely. Scrooge gave up on people and turned to money as something he could depend on.
2. The conflict is between Scrooge and himself. He has to change, or his future will be very miserable. The climax is at the end of Chapter Four, when Scrooge sees his own headstone. He now understands that all the terrible things he saw will happen if he doesn't change. Scrooge promises to change the way he lives. The main theme of the story is the idea that living and enjoying life, and being generous and kind, is much better than being cruel, selfish, lonely, and only caring about money.

APPENDIX

Dickens's Works

Novels:

1837	*The Pickwick Papers*
1837–1839	*Oliver Twist*
1838–1839	*Nicholas Nickleby*
1840–1841	*The Old Curiosity Shop*
1849–1850	*David Copperfield*
1852–1853	*Bleak House*
1855–1857	*Little Dorrit*
1859	*A Tale of Two Cities*
1860–1861	*Great Expectations*

Novellas:

1843	*A Christmas Carol*
1844	*The Chimes*

Extra Resources

Dickens and A Christmas Carol:

- http://www.victorianweb.org/authors/dickens/xmas/pva13.html
- http://www.online-literature.com/dickens/christmascarol/
- http://charlesdickenspage.com/

Victorian Literature and Culture:

- http://www.victorianweb.org/
- http://www.infoplease.com/ce6/ent/A0858005.html

Track Listings for A Christmas Carol